CRACKING THE CODE

Understanding Jesus' Parables

by LeRoy Lawson

Obtain a 64-page leader's guide to accompany this paperback.
Order number 1967 from Standard Publishing or your local
supplier.

A Division of Standard Publishing
Cincinnati, Ohio 45231
No. 40042

© 1977, The STANDARD PUBLISHING Company
a division of Standex International Corp.

Library of Congress Catalog No. 76-57045
ISBN 0-87239-125-6

Printed in U.S.A.   1977

Table of Contents

1

Where Does God's Kingdom Grow?

Matthew 13:1-23

Most of us disliked studying high-school English, especially English literature, even more especially Shakespeare. We labored over the tough words and strange sentences and grimaced in distaste as we tried to memorize some of the "important passages" assigned. We declared that, once we got out of school, we would never have another thing to do with Shakespeare.

Then, quite by accident, something unexpected happened. We saw a Shakespeare production starring a great actor, like Sir Laurence Olivier. He didn't *teach* Shakespeare to us; he pronounced Shakespeare's words and shook out his dusty poetry in dramatic action that was alive. To our surprise, we enjoyed Shakespeare.

Unfortunately, many former Sunday-school students suffered a similar experience with Jesus. They learned to quote the King James English, but not understand it; they sat through weeks and years of Sunday-school sessions taught by well-meaning but sometimes ill-prepared teachers; and they developed an abiding distaste for Jesus' teachings.

Then one day, perhaps also by accident, they turned to a parable and read the beautifully simple words of the Master Teacher, "A sower went out to sow . . ." And they heard Him for the first time. More than that, they understood!

Parables

There is no better place to begin one's study of Jesus' teaching than with His parables. The form of these elementary tales is almost as old as speaking. When a little girl asks, "Daddy, what is heaven like?" and her father carefully answers, "Well, heaven is like . . .," the chances are he's about to tell her a parable.

A parable (from the Greek *parabole,* literally a placing beside in order to compare) is one way to say "It's like . . ." A simile is a very simple expressed comparison ("Oh my love's like a red, red rose"); a metaphor is a simple implied comparison ("He's a rock, a veritable rock"). A parable also is a comparison, but longer, in narrative form. It is a story drawn from everyday experience to teach a spiritual lesson.

Upon first hearing, a parable seems to be a most obvious story. It is the story of a man sowing seeds, only some of which grow to fruition; or of a wasteful son who squanders his inheritance and returns penitently to his forgiving father; or of a good Samaritan who rescues an unfortunate robbery victim on the Jericho road. The stories are interesting in themselves, but for those who have "ears to hear," they are more than interesting; they are instructive. They have the force of an argument, compelling the hearer to nod in agreement. What happens in the story is like an important spiritual truth, which the spiritually discerning person can understand.

The Gospel parables are timeless, as relevant to our day as to Christ's. The questions they tackle are the big questions of our lives. "Who is my neighbor?" "What is the kingdom of Heaven like?" "What is the value of

6

human life?" "What is righteousness?" "How does God's judgment differ from human judgment?"

It is important to remember that Jesus is usually dealing with only one question in a parable. Beware the temptation to make every parable an allegory in which each thing that is mentioned has a specific meaning in the spiritual interpretation. Some parables are interpreted in that way. In the parable of the soils, for example, every one of the four soils stands for a specific type of hearer, the seed stands for the word, the field for the world. Most of the parables are not allegories, however, and must not be pressed to mean more than is intended. Some details of the stories may be scenery, with no deeper meaning.

We will more correctly interpret the parables if we can remember that this is a spoken form, not a literary one. The hearers would grasp the main meaning as Jesus talked, but would pay little attention to the minor details. We should do the same. As we read, we cannot help exploring the implications of these details, but we must not let our imaginations cause us to misapply the story.

The parable of the sower raises a question that we still hear in Bible classes: Why does Jesus speak in parables? An answer comes from the place of His teaching. He is not teaching in the synagogue, where Bibles are available and the people are eager to hear an explanation of a particular passage. Rather, He is strolling along the Sea of Galilee, or speaking to a crowd on a hillside, or teaching a smaller group in a crowded room of a friend's home. There He points to objects or scenes within the view of His audience, using them as homely illustrations to make Scriptural truths come alive. He translates abstract principles into concrete, compelling language.

Not everyone understands, of course. Some are too preoccupied, or too blind, or perhaps too lazy to see the spiritual truths in the parables. They do not have ears to hear. Undoubtedly Jesus tells the parable of the soils because of them.

The Parable of the Soils

One lesson is obvious from this story: the message of God's kingdom will take root and grow! Jesus began His ministry with John the Baptist's challenging message: "The time is fulfilled, and the kingdom of God is at hand; repent, and believe in the gospel" (Mark 1:15). The gospel, of course, is the good news that God so loved the world that He sent His Son to save all who would believe in Him. But by this time in Jesus' ministry the disciples are aware that not everyone hearing this message is accepting it and turning to Christ. Some reject it immediately; others follow for a while and then desert Him. Jesus is not worried by their defection; He knows that several will remain, for they genuinely want God to reign in their lives. They hear the word of the kingdom gladly, and their lives produce.

We wonder why the word of God does not rule everywhere, in all lives. The parable suggests some reasons.

Some persons do not understand. The meaning of the word does not penetrate. As seeds fail to take root in a packed pathway, the deeper significance of the word fails to find a place in their minds. They seem hardened against God's message.

Some who reject the seed fault the sower. Blaming a preacher who talks over their head, or one who preaches too much fire and brimstone, or one whose sermons contain half-lies or objectionable truths, they turn away from the church and even from the Bible. The word of truth cannot pierce their defenses. The fault, they insist, is not theirs.

The parable blames them, however. They are too hard. They may be actively opposed to God's word, or simply indifferent to any challenge to their way of life, or so calloused through their profane pursuits that they cannot feel the nudges of God any more.

8

Some cannot stand the heat. The picture is that of a thin layer of soil covering stone. Seeds can quickly take root in such soil; but young plants cannot survive the sun's beating, because the little roots have not penetrated far beneath the surface.

Just so, Jesus says, hearers of the word who have no deep roots in themselves may enjoy their newfound faith for a while, but will desert when the heat of persecution or suffering beats upon them.

Instability marks these personalities. They immediately accept the word of the kingdom, but they also *immediately* leave it when the heat is on. They eagerly seek the benefits of the Christian life, but do not want to pay the price to enjoy them. Unwilling to be deeply committed to anything, they allow no genuine conviction to take root other than the belief that nothing in the kingdom is worth their inconvenience.

Nels Ferre recounts the delightful story of a man who had enjoyed remarkable experiences of God. To preserve them for future savoring, he wrote them down. Years later he moved to another city and made known his desire for membership in a church. The minister called upon him and asked about his spiritual experience. The man smiled, eager to recount his moments with God, and disappeared to the attic to get his record. After a lengthy absence he returned, embarrassed and stammering to the minister, "The rats have eaten my spiritual experience."[1]

In this man's familiar case, no tribulation or persecution caused him to fall away, but simple neglect. The gospel had no roots in him.

Examine the membership rolls of just about any church you know. In many congregations, the inactive members outnumber the active ones. Why did they fall away? Persecution? That is doubtful, at least in American society. Tribulation? That is a little more possible, for every person experiences heartache. More than likely,

9

whatever excuse is offered, the real reason is simply "no depth of soil."

The earliest Christians faced many difficulties because of their faith in Christ. Many lost their jobs, others were disowned by their families, many others were hunted down by their governments. Some had no roots and could not stand the heat. Others persevered. To encourage believers in such times of stress the apostle Paul sent words of exhortation like these: "Therefore, my beloved brethren, be steadfast, immovable, always abounding in the work of the Lord, knowing that in the Lord your labor is not in vain" (1 Corinthians 15:58).

Some are simply preoccupied. "Thorns grew up and choked them." The seed is received, the word heard. But stronger plants, "the cares of the world and the delight in riches" overwhelm the tender young faith.

In the Sermon on the Mount, after warning His followers against the folly of accumulating treasures on earth, which can be stolen or destroyed, Jesus reminds them that "where your treasure is, there will your heart be also" (Matthew 6:21). And the treasure cannot be divided between heaven and earth: "You cannot serve God and mammon" (Matthew 6:24).

Two children in Nashville were found beaten and begging for food. They had gone all winter without coats and shoes. Neighbors had known that the girls, one twelve and the other four, had been abused for several months, but they did not want to become involved in any legal action, so they refused to help. When the girls were finally discovered by a college student who took them to the hospital, the little four-year old was given only a fifty percent chance of surviving. She had a hole in her right hip, a toe missing, and many sores. Her older sister had part of an ear missing, broken arms that had never been properly set, and scars on her neck, back, and hands.

One of the neighbors had seen the girls several months earlier. Then, too, they had been beaten. She did not report the matter to the authorities, she said, because she didn't want to have to go to court and miss work!

One whose real concern in life is money will soon find his tentative interest in spiritual matters choked out. The neighbor whose primary worry is her paycheck will naturally allow innocent children to be abused rather than forget the money in order to rescue the children.

No wonder Jesus laments, "It will be hard for a rich man to enter the kingdom of heaven (Matthew 19:23). One may have to choose between riches and Heaven.

Or one may have to choose between Heaven and some other competing interest. Dollars are not the only thorns. What is said about devotion to dollars must also be said about a single-minded pursuit of pleasure and recreation, a disproportionate delight in sex, a longing for solitude, or whatever one allows to overwhelm the pursuit of the kingdom of God.

Some are eager to hear. This is the good news of the parable. In spite of all the alluring distractions of this sinful world, some—in fact many—are open to the word of God's love. They have tried the ways of the world and found them wanting. They desire something to live for. They want to fulfill their human potential. They want God.

Through the word of God they have overcome the world's stranglehold. God is their hope. Therefore they are the hope of the church, as the church is the hope of the world. Through these believers God accomplishes His loving will on earth. Through them His kingdom comes on earth, for in them He rules and through them He reaches the lost. They produce fruit for Him in such huge amounts that they more than make up for the fruitlessness of the seeds that fall on unproductive soil.

Thanks to these producers, God's kingdom grows.

Notes

1. *Making Religion Real.* New York, Harper and Row Publishers. 1955, p. 77.

2

What Is God Like?

Luke 15

Scandalous! This man not only teaches dangerous doctrines and violates the sacred Sabbath, but He draws about himself the most disreputable assortment of human beings imaginable. He goes even further. It is bad enough that He teaches and associates with tax collectors and sinners, but He also eats with them! To sit at table with them as friends, as social equals!

The cautious religious leaders are outraged. They have always scrupulously avoided contaminating themselves by mixing with anyone who takes their religious laws lightly or who may sully their reputations for righteousness. Yet Jesus, obviously a prophet and an expert in Jewish doctrines and ethics, seems to prefer the company of the unkempt to the society of scribes and Pharisees.

So they whisper their disdain to one another. And Jesus overhears. Earlier He told His critics, while eating at the home of Levi, a hated tax collector, that as a physician He has to go to the sick (Luke 5:27-32). What He meant then is what He attempts to teach by these parables now: His choice of companions is rooted in the very nature of God. "I have been seeking out the ones you would call 'lost' because God is like this. He loves the lost!"

Simple Similes

The likeness set forth in the parables of Luke 15 could have ben summarized as follows:

"God, whom you religious leaders worship as one high and lifted up, the unutterable, pure and spotless being, is also love, and love is a verb—action, seeking, helping, forgiving, embracing. You have always seen God on a throne or in a book or in a temple. That's not all there is to Him at all, not at all. Let me tell you what God is like.

"He is like a shepherd who notices, when he counts his hundred sheep, that one is missing. He cannot rest until he has sought and found the lost one.

"He is like a poor woman who has ten precious coins and suddenly discovers one missing. She quickly lights a lamp and sweeps every inch of her dirt floor, even into the darkest corners of the dimly lit room, until she has recovered her loss.

"He is like a father who reluctantly yields to the demands of a son for his inheritance and bids farewell to the ambitious youth, but who never stops searching the horizon for the first sign of the son's return to himself.

"Do you see? You have sought to please God by your spotless robes and your rigid schedule of rituals and your disdain of lost souls. In so doing, you have missed God. He's been elsewhere, seeking those very lost ones.

Some Specifications

God is like a careful shepherd, a searching woman, a loving father. Some specifications of those likenesses are seen in what He does.

God watches over His own. A careless shepherd would not notice one missing sheep out of a hundred. But this shepherd is not careless. Nor is God. He numbers the hairs on our heads (Matthew 10:30); He feeds the birds of the air and clothes the lilies of the field, and much more clothes His people (Matthew 6:25-34). He is with His own even in the valley of the shadow of death (Psalm 23). So we Christians sing, "His eye is on the sparrow, and I know He watches me."

Listen to the testimonies of Christians, and you will hear them say, "My God is real to me. You may think this sounds irrational, but in my moments of greatest need He is always there, watching and assisting.

He is there, in the crisis, watching over His own.

God's love is not passive, however. He does not wait for floundering men and women to seek Him somehow through philosophy or religion or science, as if He were missing. Instead, *He seeks for us when we are lost.* He assumes the initiative. A coin cannot return to its owner voluntarily; a lost sheep, caught in brambles or trapped in a hole, is helpless to return. Another must seek the lost.

Jesus presents a God who cares enough to do whatever is necessary to rescue His lost ones. The cross will prove just how far God goes to save us.

It is no wonder that the Pharisees cannot understand Jesus. They have read frequently in their religious books of the virtue of repentance and the necessity of seeking God, but Jesus' teaching of a God who actively, earnestly searches for sinners, like a good shepherd looking for a lost sheep—this is a picture of God they have not yet comprehended.

Several years ago when we were camping in a strange place, our young daughter became confused and could not find her way back to our campsite. When she did not return, we became alarmed. We immediately recruited our fellow campers and began an all-out search for our lost child. How relieved we were to find her! What a party we had!

14

Only later did we realize that our anxious search for our lost child was exactly what Jesus is portraying in these parables. God anxiously seeks for us when we are lost!

That is because *God believes in our worth.* Why did we seek so energetically for our daughter? Because she is priceless to us. That, says Jesus, is why God seeks for His own. He believes in our worth—even when we don't!

We have some difficulty accepting Jesus' teaching about God in these parables because we don't think as highly of ourselves as God does of us. When we read in Psalm 8, "When I look at thy heavens, the work of thy fingers, the moon and the stars which thou has established," we honestly ask with the psalmist, "What is man that thou art mindful of him?"

The question becomes even more personal when we compare ourselves with the many great leaders and outstanding Christians beside whom we feel so useless. It is not easy to understand God's unwavering belief in our worth. We are as puzzled as the psalmist: "Yet thou hast made him little less than God, and dost crown him with glory and honor." God's evaluation of our worth makes little sense to us. But God has so loved us, the Bible affirms, that he gave His very best, His own Son, to save us.

When the prodigal son comes to himself, he thinks of his father. The son sees himself clearly: he is a foul, stinking, hungry sinner. He has abused his privileges, squandered his father's wealth, been disrespectful of his father's faith (he is feeding pigs, something no self-respecting Jew would ever do), and dishonored the family name. Yet he dares to go home. He must know that, in spite of everything, his father believes in his worth.

Furthermore, *God respects our freedom.* At least in this story, when the son demands his inheritance, the brokenhearted father does what the son wants, even though the experienced older man knows what troubles

15

his naive son will encounter. The son's values are transparent: he seeks the father's money, not the father; he prefers his freedom to his sonship.

His father does not speak a word of condemnation. He respects the son's right to be wrong. He loves his boy even when he is rejected by him. He knows that his son has to find himself. He dreads seeing his freedom turn into slavery to his own impulses, to his self-made gods. He fears what will happen to his son when those gods fail, as they must. Nonetheless, he has brought him up to be free, free even to go wrong.

He is also free to become right. He can change. He can cause the angels of heaven to burst into song (see verses 7, 10).

He has left home in freedom; he still has the freedom to return home! The gate has not been closed against him.

When he is still some distance from home, the father does exactly what the Bible teaches that God does for us: *He stoops for our sake.* The father has every right to demand apologies and penance before accepting his erring son. (What father could resist delivering a lecture on the spot!) Instead, this father rushes to meet his son, embracing and kissing him. He does not dwell on the past, does not worry about his offended dignity or paternal pride.

Thus does Jesus define grace. *Grace* basically means an undeserved favor. At this point the son has no merit to offer; he is an utter failure. The father does not demand that the son earn his way into the father's good opinion of him. He accepts the son as he is, stooping to his son's need and drawing him up again into his fellowship.

This, the apostle Paul says, is God's way. According to Philippians 2:5-11, Jesus himself was "in the form of God" but willingly empties himself of that honored estate to stoop to our level, "taking the form of a servant, being born in the likeness of men." This is a greater gift from God than we deserve. It is grace.

16

The Pharisees and scribes who cannot understand Jesus' habit of keeping bad company cannot understand the prodigal son's father, either. Such ready forgiveness, such eager embraces, while the son still smells of the pigsty!

More and More

What does God do to show His love? Just this:

He shares His best with us. The best robe, the family ring, shoes for the abused feet, and a meal of the special fatted calf. The very best!

We cannot help thinking of Matthew 6:33. "But seek first his kingdom and his righteousness, and *all these things* shall be yours as well." "These things" in this passage are food, drink, and clothing. Jesus' teaching is clear: when service to God is one's top priority, God supplies the essentials of life. But in the parable, more than the eseentials are shared with the son. He gets the best of the basics and far more.

It is easy to see God only as a great depository of fine trinkets, if we focus on the *things* the father gives. God is not, as Will Herbert reminds us, "a great cosmic public utility,"[1] dispensing material commodities with the turn of a tap.

Something greater than utility is given the son. Imagine the love, the joy, the peace that he puts on with his robe. The father shares not only his goods but his person, his steadfast love.

The ringing testimony of Christians is that they too have received the best from their Father: wealth, gifts of the Spirit, friends, stimulation, variety, meaning, hope. He shares His best with us!

Even more, *He rejoices in our company.* A spirit of celebration floods this chapter. When the shepherd finds his lost sheep, he calls his friends and neighbors to celebrate with him. Such joy must be shared!

The woman just has to call her neighbors and friends

over for a party. You cannot keep such good news to yourself.

The exultant father cannot contain his joy. He hosts a celebration to end all celebrations!

Jesus' emphasis is a bit unexpected, isn't it? We think often of our happiness in God's presence. The heart of our worship is its spirit of celebration in the presence of the Lord. We gladly heed Paul's admonition to "rejoice in the Lord always" (Philippians 4:4). The twist here is Jesus' teaching that God rejoices in us! He wants us with Him. Thus when we "come into his presence with singing" and "enter his gates with thanksgiving," God is singing with us, enjoying our company.

Not everybody is happy with the festivities. *God risks being misunderstood by His faithful ones.* In the parables, the elder brother doesn't like the party. "To think," he seems to be saying, "that I have stayed at home and denied myself of all the fun my brother has had—yet he gets all the attention!"

It hardly seems fair, does it? That is, if you look through the selfish eyes of the brother, who still has so much more than the wayward son. He possesses his inheritance, he has enjoyed his father's abiding presence. The prodigal son has returned to his father's home, but he has lost all his inheritance and all those precious years he wore away.

The older brother is not satisfied, however. He does not have the softer eyes of his father, who eagerly rejoices that his younger son is now alive to him again. The father cannot withhold himself even when the older brother— like the scribes and Pharisees for whom Jesus has told this parable—does not understand.

God is like that!

Notes

1. "The Strangeness of Faith." *Sermons to Intellectuals From Three Continents,* ed. Franklin H. Littell. New York: The Macmillan Company; London: Collier-Macmillan Ltd., © 1963, p. 35.

3

God Is Still Seeking

Matthew 22:1-14

On a warm October day a few years ago, John Hasty, a Christian college president, slipped away from a meeting in downtown Chicago to visit a stamp store for his son. He recorded his impressions of City Hall Square in his college paper.

On one edge of the square a crowd passed out handbills, chanting "Impeach Nixon Now!"

On the other side a group of Arab sympathizers clustered about a man with a bullhorn who was vigorously denouncing U.S. involvement in the Arab-Israeli war.

And of course there was also a gathering of Israeli sympathizers demanding a U.S. guarantee of guns, tanks, and airplanes to Israel to defeat the "Egyptian aggressors."

In the middle of the plaza on a small platform, a young woman shouted that at exactly 12:30 she was going to strip off her clothing, her protest against something. And she did, to the crowd's roar of approval! A team of policewomen abruptly stopped her show and escorted her into a waiting patrol car.

19

Elsewhere in the busy plaza some young men and a group of bunnies from the Playboy Club battered each other with snowballs. The snow was provided, at an announced cost of $5,000, by a portable snow machine.

While watching all these activities, Mr. Hasty became aware of some music. In the spire of Temple Church, which overlooks City Hall Square, the carillon was playing its noontime concert. Above the noise of the crowds he could hear "Jesus keep me near the cross."

"There amidst all that hate, sensuality, conflict, and wantonness," he later wrote, "was the Christian message of salvation . . . but no one was listening.

"The message was there . . . but no one was listening."[1]

The parable of the wedding feast is quite contemporary, isn't it? The feast was prepared, the message sent out, but no one was listening. "They made light of it and went off, one to his farm, another to his business."

God's Invitation

Like the parable in the last chapter, this one presents a God who is seeking His own. The elder brother refused to attend the celebration for his returned brother because of jealousy and resentment. in this parable, the father's invitation is ignored through indifference. In spite of these rebuffs, however, God still seeks.

God invites us to a celebration. The kingdom of heaven resounds with the music of festival. Remember the shepherd who found his lost sheep? The woman who recovered her misplaced coin? The father whose prodigal son came home? Their immediate impulse was to throw a party! Even the angels of heaven joined the festivities.

Even more than today, weddings in Jesus' time were occasions of celebration. Fathers saved for years to be able to provide the best food and finest hospitality for as many guests as possible. Nothing was too good for a son's marriage.

Such, says Jesus, is the atmosphere in God's kingdom.

How strange that so many people think of the Christian life as drudgery! How wrong are those who resist the church's invitation by saying, "I don't want to become a Christian yet—I'm having too much fun. I'm not ready to give this all up for the church." For the sake of a little immediate pleasure they forsake an eternal festival.

God's invitation is to a social occasion. The parable reflects the fact that our Christian faith is not a solitary experience. The kingdom of heaven is an uncomfortable place for those who want to practice their religion alone. John Wesley understood what Christians of all centuries have known: "Christianity is essentially a social religion; to turn it into a solitary religion is indeed to destroy it." The relationship of believers to each other, in fact, is so close that Jesus insisted," Whoever does the will of my Father in heaven is my brother, and sister, and mother" (Matthew 12:50).

His words give the lie to one of our popular gospel songs, "On the Jericho Road." When sung by a good male quartet, the song makes beautiful music. But it makes terrible theology:

On the Jericho Road there's room for just two:

No more and no less, just Jesus and you.

How much easier the Christian life would be if the song were true—but how much less fun!

The early Christians did not think of their relationship with Christ as "just Jesus and me." Acts 2 describes the social life of the early church. From the beginning, "they devoted themselves to the apostles' teaching and *fellowship,* to the *breaking of bread* and the prayers" (42). They "who believed were together and had all things in common" (44), they took care of anyone in need (45), they attended the temple together (46), and ate their meals in an atmosphere of celebration, "with glad and generous hearts, praising God and having favor with all the people" (46, 47).

Not a Command

The king in the parable has every right to command, of course, but he doesn't. He prefers the company of those who want to be with him.

Our King's message is an invitation, not an order. How much simpler it would be if He would command! When He only invites, He thrusts the responsibility for a decision upon us. If He would force us to do His will, we could escape the demands of maturity. But He will not decide for us.

A woman recently counseled with me about her church membership. For a long time she has been attending our church and wants to place her membership here. Her husband, who does not attend with her, has given her permission to become a member. Several times she has talked with me about it, but still she hesitates. I am convinced that if I would tell her to do so, she would, because then I would have assumed her responsibility. I can only invite, however. I cannot decide for her.

In counseling appointments, my counselees frequently ask me to tell them what to do. I dare not. I can only counsel. I must not rob them of the maturing experience of making decisions and then assuming the responsibility for the consequences of their decisions.

That's why the king only invites—He wants His friends to accept because they desire to be with Him, and for no other reason.

God allows us to accept or refuse. In the story, the first guests refuse. Some are openly hostile (as throughout Israel's history many of God's people rejected and reviled His prophets and judges), but more are simply indifferent. They can't be bothered; they have other matters to attend to.

Surely they do not understand what an awesome responsibility the king confers with the invitation. Many years ago when J. H. Jowett was preaching at Carr's Lane in Birmingham and Buckingham Gate in Westminster,

England, one of his regular followers was boasting to a friend who attended a village chapel, "I hear the great Dr. Jowett every Sunday." The perceptive villager replied, "What a terrible responsibility."[2]

It is an almost overwhelming responsibility to hear the word of God clearly transmitted by one of His messengers. One who hears the message and turns away is in peril of forfeiting the greatest celebration of his life.

But God allows us to accept or refuse, to take our destiny—and the destinies of those dependent upon us—in our own hands.

In the parable Jesus is obviously referring to the nation of Israel. They were the chosen people. They had looked forward to the Messiah's arrival. With their favored status came an enormous duty toward God. They could not be indifferent. But with indifference is precisely how they greeted the word that the time for the Messiah's wedding with His bride (the church) had arrived. Since they would not accept the king's invitation, God would have to invite others.

We like to talk about America as a favored nation also. We sing "God bless America" and fully expect Him to do so. We are a wealthy, powerful nation, the leader of free nations. What a responsibility! God has favored us, but He expects us to be good stewards of His favor. When He blesses, He gives greater care with the blessings. When He offers a place at His banquet table, He demands a responsible decision.

God will continue seeking until He finds worthy guests. Whether we accept the invitation or not, the party will go on. His eternal purposes will be fulfilled!

We may kick against God, rebel against the church, withdraw from God's presence and the friendship of His people, put our farm or business or education ahead of Him, but whatever we do, we shall not thwart God's plan to have a celebration with the people who want to be with Him.

Many years ago at a wedding reception a rude middle-aged man accosted the minister and abruptly informed him, "I don't like church and I hate preachers." Then he launched into a tirade against his parents who had forced him to attend Sunday school. He had vowed that when he became old enough to do what he wanted, he would never again attend church. And he hadn't.

The minister knew the man and his family, He knew that his marriage was in trouble and that his children were suffering from the father's adolescent rebellion. By his refusal to accept God's invitation, he had made a wreck of his personal and family life, but he hadn't hurt God or churches or preachers at all! He did not understand that in spite of his petulance, God's purposes will be fulfilled. The party will go on.

Worthy and Unworthy

The king said, "Those invited were not worthy." Then he sent his servants to bring in some of the people usually thought to be the most unworthy of all. What kind of puzzle is this?

What made the first guests unworthy? Only their refusal of the invitation. (It is true that some—those who seized and killed the servants—were guilty of rebellion, a sin as heartbreaking as indifference. As Jesus spoke these words, He may have been thinking of the destruction of Jerusalem forty years later, in A.D. 70. But most of those on the guest list simply did not care to go.)

What made the later guests worthy? Simply the fact that they accepted the invitation. No other standards applied.

The worthy guests, after all, came from the streets! They were not brought from the courts of the powerful, nor the synagogues of the learned, nor the trading houses of the rich. They came from the streets, where all kinds mingle, the richest and poorest, the mightiest and the meanest.

24

This banquet reminds us of Halford Luccock's picture of a live church: "A live church is seeking out sinners; the real calamity for a church occurs when it becomes full of 'nice' people on a 'nice' street in a 'nice' part of town. A nice little church can never be of much use in the work of the kingdom of God."[3] God has only one standard of "niceness": Will you accept My invitation?

The guests must have been surprised. Some certianly never expected to be invited. They knew themselves to be unworthy to sit at the king's table.

Some were surprised at what this event told them about the king. They had lived in awe of Him, respected him, even worshiped him, paid him his due, obeyed his directives—but they never had suspected that he was personally interested in them. The urgency with which the messengers invited them to the banquet made it very clear, however, that the king wanted them to share his joy, which could not be complete without them!

One guest was especially surprised. He must have come in contempt of the king, for he did not even bother to dress for the occasion. He was a hypocrite, coming to the feast not to honor the son or enjoy the hospitality of the king, but for unstated reasons of his own. At any rate, he was an instruder. He had not counted on the sharp-eyed vigilance of the all-seeing king. For some reason the king, so generous in his invitation, felt compelled to cast the imposter out. It is one thing to accept God's invitation; it is quite another to try to crash the gate on one's own terms!

To read this parable of Jesus is to realize that even now God is seeking guests for His table.

Notes

1. John Hasty. "Impressions." *Key to the Great Lakes Area.* Published by Great Lakes Bible College, Lansing, Michigan, 1973.

2. Quoted by Leslie J. Weatherhead. *In Quest of a Kingdom.* New York, Nashville: Abingdon Press, 1944, p. 195.

3. "Simeon Stylites," Christian Century, LXXVII, No. 11 (March 16, 1960), 335.

4

How Does Your Kingdom Grow?

Matthew 13:31-33; Mark 4:26-29

Christmas came at night. The angels sang and the star shone in the darkness; the Savior of mankind arrived in a black hour.

At every telling of the Christmas story, believers are reminded that God does not leave His people alone, but comes to them in their darkness. Into the night He brings singing; out of something very small—the birth of a baby—He builds a kingdom of power.

Growth

Thus when Jesus compares God's kingdom to the growth of a mustard seed, or a bit of leaven transforming a bushel of meal, or a seed producing a fully matured ear of corn, He can speak with authority. From His own start as a baby born of unimportant parents in an outbuilding of an inn, He has grown into the leader of a spiritual revolution.

Better than anyone else, Jesus knows God's way of turning the commonplace into the sacred. He made a manger into a bed for a king, a cross into the key to heaven's door. He also knows what His disciples cannot yet comprehend, that this small band of ordinary men to whom He is speaking will initiate a movement that will one day encompass the globe.

Do not grow weary, He exhorts them in these simple stories of hope, but remain patient while you prepare for greater days ahead. Today you are misunderstood and even despised. Endure your hardships, for though your influence seems tiny now, it is already growing into a powerful instrument for God's purposes. Only eternity will reveal the full extent of it.

Today Jesus might tell a parable of the airplane. Shortly after the turn of this century, Orville and Wilbur Wright were putting together a strange contraption in their back yard. They promised their skeptical neighbors, who scoffed like Noah's sidewalk superintendents, that their machine was going to fly. And it did! Just a few yards admittedly, but it flew. A tiny, sputtering, seemingly insignificant beginning. But now men have walked on the moon and machines have landed on Mars. We can only guess what tomorrow will bring.

There is no guess about the kingdom of God, however. We can ask Jesus how God's kingdom grows. He answers in these parables.

The Way of Growth

God's kingdom grows toward His goal. God directs that growth to fulfill His desire for mankind. A man does not scatter seed because he is interested in observing the marvels of biological change from seed to blade to ear to grain, but because he wants a harvest. God's harvest, Jesus teaches in Matthew 9:35-38, is the saving of crowds of men and women "harassed and helpless, like sheep without a shepherd."

Through their service to Christ the disciples were participating in the will of a God whose purposes cannot fail. They did not believe the twentieth-century myth of a "law of nature" that works automatically by some inner necessity apart from God.

Rather, they believed in a sovereign God who works in and through man and nature to reach His goal. Belief in God's sovereignty in creation undergirds these parables. God has created, He sustains, He orders the world. As plants grow according to His design, so does His kingdom.

God's kingdom grows in partnership with men. Somebody has to *sow* the seed, to *hide* the leaven in the meal.

We must not make too much of this point, of course, lest we skirt close to the heresy of thinking that we are adequate in ourselves. We do not make the leaven work, nor do we make seeds grow. Our scientists approach their microscopes and test tubes with awe before the mystery of life. The parables present neither the all-powerfulness of God nor the self-sufficiency of man, but a happy partnership between God's mysterious generative force and man's humble responsive labor.

One who grasps Jesus' words can never say, "Come see the tree that I have grown," or "Help yourself to the corn that I alone have brought forth." He becomes instead one of the blessed meek who thank God for the privilege of participating with Him in the growing processes.

This is the spirit that Abraham Lincoln expressed when saying goodbye to his Illinois friends at the Springfield Railroad Station. Leaving on February 11, 1861, for the White House, he said this:

> I now leave, not knowing when or whether ever, I may return, with a task before me greater than that which rested upon Washington. Without the assistance of that Divine Being, who ever attended him, I cannot succeed. With that assistance I cannot fail.[1]

This humble man's record as a self-perceived partner with God needs no further comment here, except to add

28

that his experience is another parable of growth from insignificance to importance.

God's kingdom grows by using the commonplace. Leaven and seeds—what homely illustrations! Jesus undoubtedly chooses them because they are elements of everyday life, easily understood by His audience. Like Tennyson, we can all see parables of God in the ordinary sights about us:

> Flower in the crannied wall,
> I pluck you out of the crannies;
> Hold you here, root and all, in my hand,
> Little flower; —but if I could understand
> What you are, root and all, and all in all,
> I should know what God and man is.

Jesus' talk about seeds and leaven also suggests that God does not rely upon the grand or spectacular to do His work. He does not subscribe to the American cult of bigness. He remains unmoved by trumpets and neon lights and noisy spectaculars. Remember, He changed the world with the birth of a baby, not the blast of a bomb.

God works through the commonplace. The followers of Jesus have been quite ordinary people, undistinguished in any obvious way from their contemporaries. Of course there have been a few exceptions, but by and large the kingdom has grown through the plodding labors of average men and women.

What distinguishes them from their fellows is that they hold dual citizenship, one registered in government offices, the other in the Lamb's book of life. Their double lives make them somewhat uncomfortable in this world among, as T. S. Eliot says, "an alien people, clutching their gods."[2]

One of the classic descriptions of these ordinary Christians is found in a second-century document, "The Epistle to Diognetus." Author and recipient of the letter are unknown, but the description of Christians arrests our attention. For the most part of it could have been written of today's disciples.

> Christians are not distinguished from the rest of mankind by either country, speech, or customs; the fact is, they nowhere settle in cities of their own; they have no peculiar language; they cultivate no eccentric mode of life. Certainly, this creed of theirs is no discovery due to some fancy or speculation of inquisitive man; nor do they, as some do, champion a doctrine of human origin.

Is there nothing special about these Christians? Yes, in spite of their conformity "to the customs of the country in dress, food, and mode of life in general," the letter praises "the whole tenor of their living."

> They reside in their respective countries, but only as aliens. They take part in everything as citizens and put up with everything as foreigners. Every foreign land is their home, and every home a foreign land. They marry like all others and beget children; but they do not expose their offspring. Their board they spread for all, but not their bed. They find themselves *in the flesh,* but do not live *according to the flesh.* They spend their days on earth, but hold citizenship in heaven. They obey the established laws, but in their private lives they rise above the laws.

The letter goes on to say that these Christians pay a price for their high standards.

> They love all men, but are persecuted by all. They are unknown, yet are condemned; they are put to death, but it is life that they receive. *They are poor and enrich many;* destitute of everything, they abound in everything. They are dishonored, and in their dishonor find their glory. . . .[3]

God uses such ordinary persons with their extraordinary influence to make His kingdom grow.

The Certainty of Growth

By now it is apparent that *God's kingdom grows with power.* That power is invincible, inherent in the purposes of God. This is the central teaching of the parables. The kingdom grows inevitably, certainly, constantly. It has a divine vitality, one that even the gates of hell cannot diminish.

Look at a recently paved driveway or parking lot and you will see this power. Here and there a bit of green, a tiny sprout, defying the weight of the asphalt, has quietly pushed through the resistance to reach the sunlight.

Look at a concrete wall, crumbling because a network of roots from an invincible plant has dislodged the rocks from their casement of cement.

Look at a stone catching the raindrops in its hollowed basin, yielding before the unrelenting power in the tiny water pellets that slowly but irresistibly wear away the solid rock.

Look at a massive parliamentary body, backing away from the irresistable force of a single personality totally committed to a goal.

Or consider the silent, invisible, contagious power of leaven, transforming bread dough by moving from cell to cell, fermenting change.

With these examples of quiet, unstoppable power in mind, reflect on the churches of Christ. First Jesus had but a handful of followers, to whom He opened the mysteries of the goals of God. Then, when He left them, He gave them the empowering presence of His Spirit (Acts 1:8). These men in turn gathered others around them, and the gathered Christians met in cells. Then men and women from each cell moved into the dough of society, infiltrating it with the yeast of change, and before long the little cells fermented a revolution in society.

This is how the kingdom works, like yeast, stealing quietly from person to person, social group to social group, and surely transforming them.

Fermentation takes time. The power in the kingdom seldom erupts in explosive violence. Explosions often leave piles of destruction. The work of the kingdom, however, is construction, and it takes longer to build than to destroy.

One cannot read these parables without concluding that as the kingdom of God grows, so must His churches. Evangelism (reaching out to others around us with the good news of Jesus Christ) and missions (reaching out to those beyond us with the same good news) are the means by which this kingdom grows on earth. To rethink the church's purpose on earth in light of these parables is to be reminded that

—God's purpose is rescuing the lost;

—His strategy is to work in partnership with those who believe in Him;

—His materials are commonplace events and persons;

—His assistance is an unconquerable power.

Notes

1. Quoted in Elton Trueblood, *Abraham Lincoln: Theologian of American Anguish.* New York: Harper and Row Publishers, © 1973, p. 9.

2. "Journey of the Magi."

3. "The Epistle to Diognetus." *Valiant for the Truth,* ed. David Otis Fuller, D.D. New York, Toronto, London: McGraw-Hill Book Co., Inc. © 1961, pp. 9-10.

5

The Moment to Decide

Matthew 7:24-27

> Once to every man and nation
> Comes the moment to decide,
> In the strife of Truth with Falsehood,
> For the good or evil side.

James Russell Lowell's famous lines, required memory work in high-school English classes a few years ago, emerge from the shadows of one's mind in moments of decision. At least once a year, for the New Year's resolutions ritual, we valiantly assert, "Now is the moment to decide!" We draw up our self-improvement list and pledge to be true and faithful to our promises. Then we struggle fiercely for a week or two into the new year, begin making excuses for our failures, and slip back into our familiar, comfortable ways.

It isn't that we don't believe our decisions are important. They are. It is just that self-betterment is so difficult.

The Sermon on the Mount closes with a challenge to a stronger life. "Whoever hears these words of mine *and does them* . . ." Jesus' audience has been listening intently. They try to understand the strange words Jesus is speaking, and many of them, especially the ones in earnest about building better lives, are intrigued.

But listening is not enough: *"And does them,"* Jesus continues. These are the crucial words. "You have heard my teachings. They are the materials for constructing the good life. They can resist the most violent storms that can blow your way. But they are valueless unless you *do* them."

Truth is something we do. Jesus invites His followers to act, to respond to His teachings by *doing* their truth and thereby building a solid life.

The Opportunity

"Every one then who hears these words of mine" has the opportunity to do them! Not all readers of the Sermon on the Mount would agree with Jesus that everyone hearing the words could do them, even if he wanted to.

The teachings are too impractical, some would say. You cannot expect me to go the second mile in my business, or to look at a beautiful woman without lusting, or to refrain from judging (since judging is second nature to all of us), or to turn my cheek when insulted! You are being too impractical, Lord. Our age gives us no opportunity to live as You say.

They are only for very spiritual persons, others add, thereby eliminating themselves. Jesus seems to be requiring an earth-forsaking otherworldliness, a complete divorce from the real experience of most people. "I would have to become like a holy man of India or like a Buddhist monk. There is no opportunity for me to follow Jesus' teachings—I'm not spiritual enough."

However, we cannot escape the obvious: Jesus thinks we can do His words. He challenges us—even when we don't want to accept it—to try His teachings.

He does not doubt our ability to reach the high standard of living He presents in the Sermon on the Mount. His teaching is based on His full acknowledgement of

God's grace and the Spirit's assitance. He prefaces any demands He plans with a knowledge that God will give us the help we need to grasp this opportunity. Even when He commissioned His disciples to go into all the world, He assured them of His constant help. He told them to be His witnesses in Jerusalem, Judea, Samaria, and the world; but He instructed them to await the coming of the Spirit who would guide them (Acts 1:8). When He sent them on their first preaching journey (Matthew 10), He warned them about the many trials they would experience, but eased their anxiety by assuring them that in their defenses "the Spirit of your Father (will be) speaking through you."

Even in the Sermon on the Mount, the high eternal demands are interlaced with reminders that the heavenly Father knows all our needs, including the strength to do His will. The fact that the Father will provide all we need makes it possible, then, to do Jesus' words.

The Choice

The fact that God has given us the opportunity to follow Jesus forces us to choose. Jesus has told us what we can do; what remains is for us to choose to do it. One man summarizes our situation this way: "Wisdom is knowing what to do next, skill is knowing how to do it, and virtue is doing it."[1] The conclusion of the Sermon on the Mount is thus an invitation to become virtuous.

Jesus hopes His audience will not simply admire His words. Admiration has long been a popular substitute for action; it has always been in good taste to admire Christian teachings, and the admiration costs nothing.

That reminds one of a story that made the rounds some time back. It was reported that several years ago a plow was sent to Africa and became the possession of a tribe in the interior of the continent. The tribesmen did not know what to do with the shiny object, so they constructed a pedestal, mounted the plow upon it, and worshiped it. The plow, however, had been designed to turn the soil and prepare it to produce fruit; to worship it was to pervert its purpose. Similarly, Jesus meant His teachings to be a tool to assist in producing fruitful lives; to simply admire them is to pervert them.

It is just as bad, of course, only to discuss His words. Many churches can boast of their fine Bible classes and discussion groups. They are to be commended for centering their church life upon the Word, but they need to warn the Christians who attend such studies that they are running grave risks. Many a would-be Christian builder has built his spiritual house upon the sands of discussion.

Jesus' words do not seem easy to build upon. He has spoken about meekness, mourning, turning the other cheek, going the second mile, loving one's enemies. Do these seem to be rocklike qualities? All through the sermon Jesus has contrasted His approach to life with the traditional one. Try all the ways of life you may, He seems to say, and in the end you will find that nothing comes out as solid reality but this way of mine. Everything else is sand; this is the rock. Jesus' claim would be most audacious, indeed, if it weren't so true.

In forcing us to make a decision, Jesus takes His place among many Bible teachers. From Genesis through Revelation the Word confronts us with the need to choose:

> I have set before you life and death, blessing and curse; therefore choose life, that you and your descendants may live (Deuteronomy 30:19).

> Now therefore fear the Lord, and serve him in sincerity and in faithfulness; put away the gods which your fathers served beyond the River, and in Egypt, and serve the Lord. And if you be unwilling to serve the Lord, choose this day whom you will serve (Joshua 24:14, 15).

> How long will you go limping with two different opin-
> ions? If the Lord is God, follow Him; but if Baal, then
> follow him (1 Kings 18:21).

> I know your works: you are neither cold nor hot. Would
> that you were cold or hot! So, because you are lukewarm,
> and neither cold nor hot, I will spew you out of my mouth
> (Revelation 3:15).

When General Robert E. Lee decided to surrender the
Confederate forces at Appomattox, he knew he was in for
severe criticism. One of his own officers did not understand: "Oh, General, what will history say of the surrender of the army in the field?"

Lee replied that hard things would indeed be said by
those who didn't know the overwhelming odds. But then
he explained how he had arrived at the difficult decision:
"The question is, is it right to surrender this army: If it is
right, then I will take all the responsibility."[2]

Are Jesus' words right? Then our opportunity to follow
His teachings becomes an imperative to choose to do so.
If He is right, then we bear the responsibility for building
upon Him and His words.

Do it regardless of what anyone else says.

The Test

The rains will come. Make no mistake about it. Jesus'
teachings are not designed for a protected monastic
existence. His people live in the real world, sharing men's
toil and wearing men's smell. God sends His rain upon
the just and the unjust. Whatever falls to the lot of humanity falls to Christians. They do not escape suffering;
they can, however, overcome it. The house built upon the
rock can weather rains and floods and winds.

The greatest test may not be in any calamity, but in the
grinding daily tasks that eat away at our resolve like a
cancer relentlessly devouring live cells. How we would
like to run away and hide, to escape the constant strug-

gle to stand for something and not be crushed by pressure to conform to others! "It is not difficult to get away into retirement," said the famous English preacher Frederick Robertson, "and there live upon your own convictions; nor is it difficult to mix with men, and follow their convictions; but to enter into the world, and there live out firmly and fearlessly according to your own conscience, that is Christian greatness."[3]

More often than not, however, we think of the storms in more catastrophic terms: severe illness, bereavement, financial reverses, loss of job. We fear and hate these afflictions; they violate our definition of the good life. They make us doubt the existence of God, or at least of a loving God. We resist the conclusions of the world's great thinkers, that through suffering comes wisdom. God's own way of showing His acceptance—dare we say approval?—of suffering was to allow His Son to experience its pangs to the fullest.

The apostle Paul, no stranger to suffering, came to this conclusion: "We know that in everything God works for good with those who love him, who are called according to his purpose" (Romans 8:28). And later, "If God is for us, who is against us?" (Romans 8:31). And still later, "For I am sure that neither death, nor life, nor angels, nor principalities, nor things present, nor things to come, nor powers, nor height, nor depth, nor anything else in all creation, will be able to separate us from the love of God in Christ Jesus our Lord" (Romans 8:38, 39).

So let the floods come.

The Consequence

"Truth or Consequences," a quiz program that ran for many years on radio and then moved to TV, took delight in forcing participants to tell the truth or take the consequences. On the program, the consequences were a lot more fun than the truth. In life, the reverse is true. "The wages of sin is death," the Bible warns. The consequences of building on the sands of selfishness or materialism or popularity—the list is nearly endless, isn't it?—are death.

Earlier in this century one of the finest beach resorts in Oregon was called Bay Ocean. The resort was located on a peninsula that jutted out between Tillamook Bay and the Pacific Ocean. In its heyday, Bay Ocean boasted a fine hotel, a beautiful indoor seawater swimming pool (the natatorium), and a glittering host of tourists every summer season. Its bustling chamber of commerce encouraged the residents to put up signs inviting the visitor to "Watch Bay Ocean Grow."

If you were to visit Bay Ocean today, you would drive west from Tillamook along the bay to where the road turns north onto the peninsula. A new road is there, but Bay Ocean is gone. What remains of the peninsula is an isolated strip of sand. Sand is all the peninsula has ever been, even in its greatest days. Slowly, inexorably, the mighty ocean ate away at the coastline, swallowing huge loads of sand and then, one by one, the motels, the cabins, the hotel, even the natatorium.

All up and down the Oregon coast are buildings of every kind that have weathered fierce Pacific storms. They still stand, while Bay Ocean has disappeared. They are built upon rocks!

The parable concludes, then, with an implied warning similar to that of Paul's in Galatians 6:7: "Do not be deceived; God is not mocked, for whatever a man sows, that he will also reap."

As we sow, so shall we reap.

As we build, so shall we live.

Decisions have consequences.

Notes

1. David Starr Jordan, *Reader's Digest,* August 1960. p. 193.

2. Elton Trueblood, *The Life We Prize.* New York: Harper and Row, © 1951, pp. 148-149.

3. James R. Blackwood, *The Soul of Frederick W. Robertson.* New York and London: Harper and Row, © 1947, p. 131.

6

Counting the Cost
Matthew 13:44-46

You wouldn't build a tower without first estimating the cost to be certain you would finish the job, would you?

No king would march off to war against another king without first assessing the odds against him, would he?

In the same way, Jesus instructs His disciples in Luke 14:25-33, you must be prepared to pay the price to be His follower. "Whoever does not bear his own cross and come after me, cannot be my disciple." To bear a cross for Christ means simply that nothing else, not even affection for intimate family members, can interfere with one's service to the Master.

Discipleship cannot be taken lightly. It is not merely belief (that is, an intellectual assent to some proposition), but it is commitment (belief plus work plus sacrifice plus unswerving steadfastness).

This talk of crosses and sacrifices intimidates the cautious, however. Of course one is prepared to pay the cost of building a tower, or of winning a partial victory. But this talk of carrying a cross is another matter. Why should everything have to be given up for discipleship? Is it worth the cost? Jesus' answer is an enthusiastic yes. It is worth all it costs, and more.

Christians are willing, therefore, even eager, to pay the cost of discipleship because the kingdom of Heaven is more than carrying a cross. It is joy.

The parables of the treasure and the pearl of great price are about that joy.

If the kingdom of Heaven is like a treasure, discipleship is like the supreme joy of the man who finds it and eagerly sells everything he has in order to buy the field and claim the treasure, or like the man who impoverishes himself in order to claim the peerless pearl—or like the apostle Paul who forgot every other claim to his attention in order to concentrate solely on his life's goal, "the prize of the upward call of God in Christ Jesus" (Philippians 3:14).

It is true that the parables of the treasure and the pearl confront the Christian with the staggering cost of discipleship, demanding the sale of everything in return. They also propose that what is gained is priceless, to be valued above everything else in this world.

To Be Found

The kingdom of heaven is a treasure waiting to be found. It is sometimes found quite by accident. The man is at work, cultivating a field. He's not at prayer, not feeling particularly religious. He is undoubtedly surprised to discover, in the routine cousre of his daily work, riches so great that his life can never be the same. His surprise corresponds to the experience of many who find, far away from any formal worship, the blessings of the gospel coming to them from a friend or fellow-worker. God often startles by disclosing His spiritual treasures in ordinary human experiences: a chance reading of a Gideon Bible in a motel room in a lonely city, a casual conversation with a friend, a television program. As a result, those who most quickly understand God—like those who most

41

quickly grasped the meaning of Jesus' parables—are not always the "religious types" we might expect, but quite ordinary "non-religious" people who are surprised to find God's truth in Jesus and His love reaching out to them.

On the other hand, the merchant is actively seeking for fine pearls. His discovery is no accident, but the result of a concentrated search. He knows where to find them, how to spot the counterfeits, what price to pay. He is like a genuinely religious person who has devoted years to the study of great religions and philosophies, actively seeking God. Having found the truth in Jesus Christ, he willingly forsakes his former pursuits in order to devote himself to the Master.

It happens either way. Some are surprised by the gospel in the course of everyday activities, and others discover it after long and methodical search. The point of the parables is not the happenstance of the discovery, but the value of the find. Paul calls the treasure "the riches of his grace which he lavished upon us" (Ephesians 1:7, 8), or again "the riches of his glorious inheritance in the saints" (Ephesians 1:18).

To Be Chosen

Furthermore, it is a treasure waiting to be chosen. Not everyone recognizes the worth of the pearl. To an untrained eye, it may seem only slighty bigger or somewhat better than another.

A cynical eye that has been disappointed before can easily doubt that this find is all it appears to be, and refuse to pay the price for it. After all, as Shakespeare's *Prince of Morocco* discovered to his dismay, "all that glitters is not gold." Many prospectors have lost their shirts for fool's gold.

The truth is that many, for whatever reasons, have turned their backs upon genuine treasures. The value was there, but the treasure was not chosen.

Huck Finn in Twain's *Tom Sawyer* ponders just such a problem. He decides forever against right living. He rejects it for a reason seldom admitted. "Well, then, what's the use of learning to do right when it's so troublesome to do right and ain't no trouble to do wrong?" The finder of a treasure may go to considerable trouble to buy the field, but he feels that the value of the field makes the effort worthwhile. Of such value, Jesus says, is the kingdom. But only those who choose the treasure themselves will enjoy the treasure.

The treasure is not the only thing of value, of course. The man has enough valuables to buy a field; the merchant enough to purchase the pearl of great price. Jesus does not present the kingdom of Heaven as the only good thing in the world. There are many goods; the kingdom is the one best.

Not everyone can discern its value, however. To one whose aim in life is to "eat, drink, and be merry" the pearl is hardly worth the price. C. S. Lewis says that there are really only two kinds of people in the end: "those who say to God, 'Thy will be done,' and those to whom God says, in the end, 'Thy will be done.' "[1] Those who are determined to do their own will can never purchase the pearl. They will never choose it.

One thing is certain. Anyone finding the treasure is confronted with a decision. He is like a traveler who comes to a fork in the road: he must take one way or the other; he cannot have both. The pearl merchant must decide. Does he want the pearl? Will he pay the price?

To Be Purchased

The treasure has to be purchased. This does not at all contradict the sublime truth that eternal life is a free gift from God (Romans 6:23). Rather, it adds another sublime truth. The kingdom of Heaven is not only something you believe in; it is something to which you give yourself, heart and soul and mind and strength.

43

Ralph Waldo Emerson states the choice in these stark terms: "God offers to every man the choice between truth and repose. Take which you will, you can never have both."[2] Karl Barth, one of the twentieth century's leading theologians, had to take his choice in the midst of his successful teaching career. As a pastor and professor, Barth undoubtedly assumed his life would be quietly tranquil, his attention divided between his students and his books. Such was not to be, however, when Hitler became Germany's dictator. Barth refused to open his classes in Bonn with the mandatory "Heil Hitler!" Neither could he be forced to swear his unconditional allegiance to the dictator. So he was dismissed from his teaching assignment and expelled from Germany.[3]

Throughout history Christian martyrs have similarly made their choice between truth and ease. They bought the treasure of truth—then paid the price for it.

John Bunyan pays his tribute to these valiant souls in *Pilgrim's Progress*. On his journey to the Celestial City the pilgrim Christian meets Worldly Wisdom, who tries to dissuade him from continuing his pilgrimage. "I am older than thou; thou art like to meet with, in the way which thou goest, wearisomeness, painfulness, hunger, perils, nakedness, sword, lions, dragons, darkness, and, in a word, death, and what not. . . . And why should a man so carelessly cast away himself by giving heed to a stranger (and going on)?"

Christian's response testifies to the value he places upon the kingdom of Heaven, for in that kingdom he will be free from his burden of sin and guilt. Nothing else matters. "Why, sir, this burden upon my back is more terrible to me than all these things which you have mentioned: nay, me thinks I care not what I meet with in the way, if so be I can also meet with deliverance from my burden."

That is the price to be paid: to be able to say "nothing else matters." For Christian, to be rid of the burden of his sins and guilt was the supreme treasure. He would do whatever he had to do to be free from it.

But this negative note is not the tone of the parables.

To Be Enjoyed

The treasure is to be enjoyed. "In his joy" the man sells everything to obtain the treasure. It is to be relished for its own sake. Nothing else on earth is its equal.

Ask anyone what his chief goal in life is, and the chances are strong that his response will be happiness. Long ago the famed philosopher Aristotle stated as an obvious fact that we want happiness more than anything else. We will do practially anything to obtain it.

Unfortunately, it seems to be an elusive target. Perhaps so many fail to achieve it because they have not asked themselves the two questions that every counselor must eventually ask his counselees:

1. *What do you really want in life?* (That is, what would make you happy? Would the kingdom of Heaven, the rule of God in your life, be the supreme treasure for you?)

2. *What are you willing to give up to get what you want?* (That's the price to be paid. Whatever you call happiness—fame, fortune, popularity, power, marital or family success, pleasing God, whatever—will force you to forsake some other desires. There is no happiness without the sacrifice. Will you give up whatever keeps you from the treasure?)

When these questions are faced, the choices selected, the sacrifices made—then the treasure is yours.

The kingdom of heaven is to be enjoyed!

Notes

1. C.S. Lewis: *The Great Divorce* (Copyright 1946 by Macmillan Publishing Co., Inc., renewed 1974 by Alfred Cecil Harwood and Arthur Owen Barfield).

2. Quoted in Leslie Weatherhead, *The Christian Agnostic.* Hodder and Stroughton, © 1965, p. 278.

3. See David L. Mueller, *Karl Barth,* © 1972, p. 43. Used by permission of World Books, publisher, Waco, Texas.

7

The Gifts of God
Luke 11:5-13

These two parables have the same message: "How much more will the heavenly Father give." Prayer is not a futile exercise, an empty ritual. In teaching His disciples to pray what we call the Lord's Prayer, Jesus encourages them to ask as well as to praise: "give us," "forgive us," "lead us" (Luke 11:1-4). The parables following His instructions reassure the timid disciples that persistent, urgent requests are no insult to God.

A Low-level Beginning

Jesus begins on the lowest level, with a story about a neighbor who is not like God at all. He reminds us that someone as different from God as a grumpy neighbor, abruptly awakened at midnight by the loud clamor of a friend's shouts, will give his petitioner what he wants just to shut him up, if for no other reason. Persistence (or importunity, as Jesus calls it) pays off.

It is a vivid story. A traveler arrives late at night after walking many miles in the dark to avoid the burning Palestinian sun. He does not worry about his food and lodging, because he can expect his host to provide generously for him. He knows the rule of hospitality among the Jews, a sacred duty enjoined among members of the nation. Even though he arrives late and unexpected, his host must still provide for him.

But the host is embarrassed. He has nothing to offer. Although he hates to awaken his neighbor, he goes next door and asks for help. (By the way, we note that the host knows where to go. He relies upon his neighbor, assured that if he has any provisions he will not be loath to share them. When we pray, we do not address ourselves to Somebody-or-other, Whatever-God-may-be. Prayer is to one we know is there, who has what we need and is willing to provide for us.) The host calls his neighbor Friend: and friend he must be, for the caller is not put off by brusque words, even when the sleepy man tells him to go away. He knows his friend will help him once he understands the severity of his need. So he explains again, and perhaps again, until the exasperated neighbor has no choice but to give him what he wants.

There is undoubtedly a bit of turmoil within the neighbor's house, too. He says his children are in bed with him, and quite literally they are. Palestinian houses are small, with all the family sleeping together in one room. Everyone, then, is disturbed by the noise. The father has no choice but to quiet his insistent neighbor so his family can get back to sleep.

Jesus would not have us believe that God is like the reluctant neighbor, but that persistence like the importunate neighbor's will be rewarded. If it achieves its goals in such everyday matters as borrowing from a neighbor, how much more will it reward those who pray to God!

Very often, when I am frustrated in one of my writing or work projects, I am tempted to quit. But I usually don't—not because I am remarkably tenacious in applying myself to problems, but because I can never get out of earshot of my dad, who said to me more often than I can

47

remember in my youth, "If it's not worth finishing, it's not worth starting." So to this day it pains me to see unfinished projects. On the other hand, nothing gives me any more pleasure than seeing the results of sticking to a project.

Ask any outstanding achiever in sports, or the arts, or literature, or business, or any other sphere of acitvity, explain the secret of his success. Almost without exception he will give the credit not to any inspiration or genius but to plodding, persistent hard work.

That's what Jesus is illustrating about prayer. In the midnight conversation between the neighbors, effective prayer is shown to be consistent, insistent, even urgent. The man asks out of embarrassment; he should have been prepared. He asks with determination; he will not give up until his friend helps him. And one more important observation: he asks for the sake of someone else. When love for another dictates our prayers, they cannot be uttered casually.

Such prayers are answered. When one asks persistently, he receives. God rewards our importunate requests according to His understanding of our real needs. Therefore, "Ask, and it will be given you; seek, and you will find: knock, and it will be opened to you." How Jesus can speak so confidently of God's generosity He makes clear in the next parable.

A High-level Comparison

In the following verses, Jesus moves to the highest level of comparison. God can be counted on, Jesus assures His disciples, because He is like a father to a son. No earthly father would cruelly deceive a son by slipping him a poisonous snake when he asks for a fish, or a scorpion in place of a requested egg. Even though men are more to be characterized by the evil they do to one another than by the good, no worthy father would deliberately withhold from his son when he can give the good

48

things the son asks. Surely the Father in Heaven is as good as any father on earth.

If in praying we are to ask with the urgency of the host with an unexpected guest, then in expectancy we are to await God's answer like a son anticipating the generosity of a good father.

In commenting upon God's generosity, Helmut Thielicke has observed, "Jesus never said (as can be easily seen!) that the one who asks his Father for bread shall receive bread in all circumstances. Rather, he only said that under no circumstances shall he receive a stone. By that he means that the Father will never let us down."[1]

It is equally interesting to note that the son has asked for bread and eggs, not Danish pastries and filet mignon. The needs are basic. Nowhere in His teaching does Jesus promise us all that we may wish for, but instead He is confident that God will provide for our necessities. The son, perhaps somewhat awed by his father, approaching him timidly yet trustingly, has thought through his request. He does not act the spoiled darling. He needs something to eat, nothing more. While he may have fantasies of banquet halls and luxuries, he asks for what he needs. That may be a difference between *wishing* and *praying.*

Nonetheless, other Scriptures confirm that God's gifts are many, and they are not just the essentials.

In Matthew 6:33 Jesus does promise the basic necessities to those who "seek first his kingdom and his righteousness." Romans 6:22, 23 places no limits on God's goodness, however, not even the boundary of time: "But now that you have been set free from sin and have become slaves of God, the return you get is satisfaction and its end, eternal life. For the wages of sin is death, but the free gift of God is eternal life in Christ Jesus our Lord."

Furthermore, while still remaining on this earth God's children are promised many gifts. In Romans 12 these are listed as being given individually to members of the body of Christ, the gifts being prophecy, service, teaching, exhorting, liberality, assistance, mercy, etc. First Corinthians 12 lists utterance of wisdom, utterance of knowledge, faith, healing, miracles, prophecy, discernment, and tongues as gifts that various individuals have received.

Were we to prepare our own catalogue of God's gracious gifts to us, how long it would be! We'd have to begin with the experience of God's love and the tremendous relief of forgiveness of sins. We would then add the freedom we enjoy in Christ, the hope with which we look toward tomorrow, our deep friendships in the church, the sense of purpose and meaning our lives have acquired. How long would be the catalogue!

The Greatest Gift

Obviously God does not limit His answers to the specifics of our requests. This parable offers the greatest gift of all: God's Holy Spirit. "If you then, who are evil, know how to give good gifts to your children, how much more will the heavenly Father give the Holy Spirit to those who ask him."

Nothing is said in the parable about asking specifically for the Holy Spirit. In Matthew's version (7:11) the Spirit is not even mentioned. ("How much more will your Father who is in heaven give good things to those who ask him!") Matthew deals with the specifics; Luke captures the essence of so much of Jesus' teaching. Yes, you will receive good things, but more importantly you will have the Source of all good things with you.

Jesus has now reached the high peak of these two parables on prayer. What begins with a pounding on the door in an emergency concludes with the true essence of our relation with God, a personal, continued abiding in His presence through His Spirit.

When my wife and I were in Switzerland in 1972, the Volkswagen microbus in which we and our six collegiate companions were traveling developed brake troubles. Unfortunately, the problem confronted us when we were in the countryside, camping in a little village several miles from the nearest VW dealearship. Even more unfortunately, my broken German was quite insufficient to explain the complications on our mechanical difficulties to anyone, so I feared driving alone to a service garage. I felt quite helpless. Then to my relief I learned that a Dutch gentleman was camping in the same spot with us, and he could speak satisfactory English. I asked him for directions to the next town, explained my difficulty, and solicited his opinion on how I should negotiate with a mechanic. He answered all my questions and I began to relax somewhat. Then he did something very generous. He offered to accompany me to the town and translate for me. He left his family and devoted the morning to my problem. I need not tell you with what gratitude I still think of him.

It is one thing to receive specific answers to specific questions. How much better it is to have the abiding presence of a friend! So the heavenly Father gives His Holy Spirit to abide with His children.

We should note here, however, that the Holy Spirit is a gift that God cannot give without our wanting it. My Dutch friend could offer to accompany me to the garage, but would not do so unless I accepted his offer. God cannot, by His own designs, thrust Himself upon us. He is as near as our prayers but as aloof as our independence. A father can give his son egg and bread and toys and money and every*thing* else, but he cannot give himself to his son unless the son allows him to.

How painful it is for parents when their children go through the difficult teenage years! That age is often characterized by adolescent rebellion, withdrawal, and independence as the psyche makes the perilous journey from childhood to maturity. The wise parent watches and waits, accepting rebuffs to proffered help, hoping for the day when the child will again accept not only parental money and presents, but also parental love and presence. On that day the child will receive the greatest gift a parent can give.

"How much more will the heavenly Father give the Holy Spirit to those who ask him!"

Notes
1. The Meaning of Prayer," *Twenty Centuries of Great Preaching.* Clyde E. Fant, Jr. and William M. Pinson, Jr., eds., © 1971. XII, 236. Used by permission of World Books, publisher, Waco, Texas.

8

Who Is My Neighbor?
Luke 10:25-37

In the beginning, the religious impulse is selfish.

"What shall I do to inherit eternal life?" The lawyer is not the only one who has asked Jesus this question. The rich young ruler asked the same one (Mark 10:17). In both cases the emphasis is upon the *I*. "What shall *I* do to inherit eternal life *for me?*"

Perhaps this is the basis of human religious quest. Death looms before us as an awful enemy, cutting human endeavor short too quickly, before we are ready. Therefore the sages have sought to find the gateway to eternity, seeking to save themselves from oblivion. Jesus does not fault either the rich young man or the lawyer for desiring to live forever. In both cases, however, he exposes their self-centeredness.

The lawyer is a theologian. As an expert in the Old Testament, he must flinch as Jesus touches him at his most vulnerable spot. He attempts to justify himself, deflecting the implied criticism with the face-saving question, "And who is my neighbor?"

As a lawyer he already knows the answer to his question about eternal life. He is well acquainted with Deuteronomy 6:5 ("and you shall love the Lord your God with all your heart, and with all your soul, and with all your might") and Leviticus 19:18 ("you shall love your neighbor as yourself"). He cannot have studied these verses without comprehending that in them is the foundation of the Jewish faith.

Perhaps he is searching for something new, like the mysterious utterings of a Hindu guru or the popular marvels of transcendental meditation. To hear some dazzling departure from his inherited faith may be his goal, or possibly he hopes to draw from Jesus some heresy with which he can expose the Master as a fraud. Whatever his reason for asking, he receives an answer that makes him squirm—because Jesus tells him nothing he does not already *know,* but something he is not *doing.*

The Real Problem

The lawyer's problem, Jesus knows, is not that he cannot answer his own question; the difficulty is not one of knowledge, but of works. The parable vividly illustrates that famous paragraph from James:

> What does it profit, my brethren, if a man says he has faith but has not works? Can his faith save him? If a brother or sister is ill-clad and in lack of daily food, and one of you says to them, "Go in peace, be warmed and filled," without giving the things needed for the body, what does it profit? So faith by itself, if it has no works, is dead (James 2:14-17).

Jesus moves quickly from the lawyer's intellectual understanding of the Bible's teaching to the test of action. "You have answered right; do this, and you will live." You have sought eternal life mentally. You have studied your Scriptures and assented to their truth. One thing remains: you must *will to do,* that is, you must put into action the faith you claim.

"And who is my neighbor?" The lawyer's motive in asking this question is transparent. As his mouth utters these words his heart must be saying, "I know what I must do, but I need an excuse for not doing it. Here is a possible alibi: I'll make Him define the word *neighbor.*"

Jesus does not take the bait. Any general definition would still allow a legalist to miss the point and escape his obligation. Instead, Jesus tells one of His most forceful and disturbing stories. His audience cannot misunderstand.

Who My Neighbor Is Not

"Who is my neighbor?" The parable certainly suggests who my neighbor is not.

He is not necessarily a religious professional. The priest and the Levite represent such professionals. In Christ's day they were the living symbols of Judaism. They acted as national watchdogs over morality, as legalists of Scriptural interpretation, presiders at the rituals. To think of the holy was to think of them. That the Scriptures portray them as the chief enemies of Jesus' ministry is proof of their importance as guardians of the faith. His easy association with society's bad elements and His hypnotic authority over crowds threatened their position at the pinnacle of their culture. It is easy to imagine the twinkle in Jesus' eye as He portrays His antagonists in this story as too hurried, or too preoccupied, or too afraid, or too insensitive to human suffering to assist the battered victim along their pathway.

The irony of the story is especially delicious when we recall that many priests and Levites in the audience had repeatedly exhorted their flocks to "love your neighbor as yourself." When put to the test, Jesus implies, these teachers would flunk.

The acid test of devotion to God, instead of being faithfulness to ritual or fervency in prayer to God, is one's love of his neighbor. Nothing in the story is said about the

Samaritan's religious convictions. Nothing is said about the victim's faith, either. If he and his rescuer discussed religion is not disclosed. If the Samaritan preached to the victim, Jesus leaves that fact out of the story. What is important at this point is the practical act of love.

No more devoted religious leader can be found in the New Testament than Saul of Tarsus (Acts 9). Of himself he testified, "According to the strictest party of our religion I have lived as a Pharisee" (Acts 26:5). His religious zeal drove him to devour the Scriptures and uphold every letter of the Jewish law, worshiping God fervently with all his heart and strength. But no one could have accused Saul of Tarsus of loving his neighbor, especially if the neighbor was a Christian. Then Saul met the risen Jesus on the road to Damascus. Agonizing thought and further revelations followed, and Saul became the great apostle Paul. Knowing Jesus had changed this hate-filled zealot into one who so understood the meaning of loving one's neighbor that he could write the Christian masterpiece of love, 1 Corinthians 13. The religious leader had to be converted into a neighbor.

My neighbor is not just the man next door. The lawyer is toying with the literal definition of neighbor as "one who is nearby, adjacent to." By so limiting his definition he is able to restrict his charitable impulses.

Jesus knocks the walls out of that definition. The Samaritan is on a journey, far from his home, deep in dangerous territory. He is traveling alone. No one will know whether he pauses to help the victim or not. And if another traveler should see him pass by, the observer could offer no word of criticism. In fact, he might commend him for acting so prudently. It is unwise to stop where robbers are plentiful; it is foolish to risk one's life for the sake of a stranger.

But love is risky business. Our neighbor is where we find him, not just conveniently residing in the safe little house next door.

No wonder this parable has had such a disturbing impact upon our mobile society. We can travel our great distances to get away from our everyday obligations, only to discover upon our arrival that a neighbor is there, one we have never met before. The neighbor may be in the city we visit along the way, in a car stranded beside the freeway, in the apartment thirteen floors overhead, or in the pushing line in a crowded grocery store. He may work at the bench next to me or ride alone in the subway.

My neighbor does not have to be a person like me, either. Samaritans and Jews were racial and religious enemies. There was no social intercourse between them. Jesus' Jewish listeners were not prepared to hear Him call a Samaritan their neighbor.

Could the author of the Christian faith, which teaches that God gave his Son for all the world, have said a Samaritan was not a neighbor to a Jew? Can we read this parable today without realizing that in it Jesus cuts to the heart of all human prejudice?

In the midst of the bitter racial hostilities in Rhodesia in the summer of 1976, four hundred black and a hundred white Christian leaders of the strife-torn nation met in Bulaway for the Rhodesian Congress on Evangelism in Context. It was a tense seven-day meeting. Many black participants, reacting to the white government's segregationist rulings, said, "I *can't* love whites." "You must," replied Ralph Bell, an American black who gave several major addresses at the congress. "That is the way of the cross."[1]

Thus even in the twentieth century many Christians have had difficulty grasping this meaning of the cross. In Christ there is neither Jew nor Samaritan, just as "there is neither slave nor free, there is neither male nor female; for you are all one in Christ Jesus" (Galatians 3:28). Whatever prejudices we may have harbored before we were brought beneath the cross have been dissolved in the unifying blood of Christ.

My neighbor is not just humanity in general. Many Christians embrace the doctrine of the necessity of doing good to humanity in general, but remain heartlessly unloving to a specific person of another color or social group.

Jesus does not let the lawyer off the hook by answering in broad generalities about good feelings to man-in-general based upon some vague concept of the brotherhood of man. How much easier it would be for us if He did! Our problem is not in loving humanity, but in loving specific persons whose ways are not our ways.

Does my love extend to persons whom I fear? whom I resent? whom I don't like? Do I talk of my love for God and withhold my love for one of His creatures?

Who My Neighbor Is

Who is my neighbor? That is the lawyer's question, but through this parable Jesus subtly changes it to a more penetrating one: To whom am *I* a neighbor?

That is the question Jesus answers, and His answer is very plain: the one who shows mercy is the neighbor.

My neighbor, then, is potentially anyone who needs my help. The Samaritan becomes a neighbor to the victimized traveler simply by responding to his need. No, that is not quite accurately stated. He does not *simply* respond. He does what is necessary to assist the man—he goes to him, cleans the wounds with oil and wine, binds them, takes him to an inn—then does still more. He stays and nurses him as long as he can, prepays his bill in the inn so he can have further rest, and guarantees that the man will receive care as long as necessary. Such full helpfulness is far from simple.

The parable's key word for the Samaritan is *compassion.* When he sees the man's pitiful condition he is moved deeply, feeling within himself the victim's pain. The fullness of this word becomes evident when we turn to some of its other uses in the New Testament. *Compas-*

sion describes the father's feeling upon first seeing his returning prodigal son (Luke 15:20); with *compassion* Jesus looks upon the multitudes before healing them (Matthew 14:14). It is His *compassion* that compels Him to call for more workers to save lost men and women (Matthew 9:36). *Compassion* is also the word of the father begging Jesus to heal his demon-driven son (Mark 9:22, King James Version: "have compassion on us").

Jesus demands more of His audience than compassion, however, and the lawyer knows it. He recognizes that the real neighbor is the one who shows *mercy,* which is compassion in action. "God, who is rich in mercy . . . made us alive." So says Paul in Ephesians 2:4, 5. "God our Savior . . . saved us, not becuase of deeds done by us in righteousness, but in virtue of his own *mercy*" (Titus 3:5). Using God's compassionate action as the example, and relying upon the teachings of the Old Testament, Jesus instructs His critics, "Go and learn what this means, 'I desire *mercy,* and not sacrifice'" (Matthew 9:13).

The Bible does not offer a greater illustration of the meaning of human mercy than this parable. As Jesus instructs the lawyer to do what he knows (verse 28), so He speaks beyond the lawyer to all His disciples to urge us to *do* what we *feel.* Loving one's neighbor begins with a feeling of compassion; it expresses itself in acts of mercy.

My neighbor, therefore, is one who receives my love. A new bond is established, a new relationship formed when the needy receives mercy. Those who were before only potentially neighbors have been joined, with the needy one actually receiving from the one needing to give.

"Love is a doorway," reads one definition, "through which the human soul passes from selfishness to service and from solitude to kinship with all mankind."[2]

But what if I do not feel like loving my neighbor? Someone will surely ask this. One cannot force love, of course, if love is simply a feeling. But if it is a feeling issuing in action, then what is imperative is the action, not the emotion. Says C. S. Lewis:

> Thus the rule for all of us is perfectly simple. Do not waste time bothering whether you "love" your neighbor; act as if you did. As soon as we do this we find one of the great secrets. When you are behaving as if you loved someone, you will presently come to love him.[3]

Your acts of mercy will pave the way for your growing feelings of compassion.

The Answer

Who then, is the neighbor?

He is one who cannot stand to see another suffer.

He is one who cannot enjoy his prosperity while another is deprived.

He is one who knows he is needed and does not shrink from offering what he has.

He is one who develops his will to do right and is thus guided by principle rather than emotions.

He is one who cares.

He is one who cannot pass by.

Notes

1. *Christianity Today.* June 4, 1976, p. 51.

2. Quoted in Karl Ketcherside, *The Parable of Telstar and Other Talks.* St. Louis: Mission Messenger, n.d., p. 60.

3. C.S. Lewis: *Mere Christianity* (Copyright 1943, 1945, 1952 by Macmillan Publishing Co., Inc.).

9

To Believe Is to Obey

Matthew 21:28-32

This brief parable and the one following in verses 33-41 are spoken to a particular audience. The Jewish religious leaders are once again attacking Jesus, questioning His authority and resenting His popularity with crowds. "By what authority are you doing these things?" they demand. Knowing their motive, Jesus refuses to respond to them directly. His parables, however, leave no doubt in anyone's mind about what His answer is.

This chapter will concentrate on the brief story of two sons, because even though its immediate meaning is apparent, the implications of the parable command our attention.

The Sons

The one son represents the leaders of Israel, those who claim to be God's very own people, ready to do His bidding. To God they say, "I go, sir"; but they do not go. The other represents those whom the leaders call sinners, all who live outside the strictly-drawn boundaries of Jewish religion. They formerly made no pretense of being religious: both in their attitude toward formal religion and in their moral behavior they said "I will not" to God. Their lives changed, however, when they heard and believed John the Baptist (see Matthew 3:1-10).

The parable comments, then, both upon the religious leaders' rejection of God's will and upon the sinners' unexpected acceptance of it.

Jesus emphasizes the fact that accepting God's word is not a matter of professing a willingness to obey, but of actually *obeying*. "Which of the two *did* the will of his father?" is the key question. Obedience is what the father asks, not courtesy, for obedience is the genuine expression of faith. Dietriech Bonhoeffer summarizes the relation between belief and obedience quite abruptly: "Only he who believes is obedient, and only he who is obedient believes." Is this another way of stating James 2:26? "For as the body apart from the spirit is dead, so faith apart from works is dead."

Questions

The very brevity of the parable raises several questions that bear on the kinship of believing and obeying.

The first question comes from Jesus' application of His parable. *Why does He favor tax collectors and prostitutes?* His position seems unfair: "Truly, I say to you, the tax collectors and the harlots go into the kingdom of God before you."

The Jewish leaders hardly seem that bad, do they? They meant well. They assumed the lonely burden of leadership; they applied themselves rigorously to the discipline of their laws. They fearlessly stood for God and righteousness in a sinful world. The tax collectors, on the other hand, had shamelessly sold their integrity by collecting the hated Roman taxes from their fellow Jews, lining their pockets at the expense of their own people. Nothing needs to be added here, either, about the social scorn heaped upon women who sold their bodies.

Jesus never ceases to amaze even twentieth-century readers by His daring reversal of our expectations. We might have thought the chief priests and elders, who seemed so earnest in their devotion to God, should be reprimanded by Jesus for their spiritual pride, perhaps, but not placed below such obvious sinners.

By extension, is Jesus suggesting that today's social reprobates may have a higher place in God's affection than preachers and elders in the church? How should we understand Him?

Jesus is not attacking genuine efforts to please God, of course: but He is faulting those who parade as God-pleasers while failing to practice what they preach. The Jewish leaders to whom Jesus is speaking say they will obey God, but do not. The tax collectors and harlots, on the other hand, once refused God's requests: but when confronted with John's word of truth, they repented of their stubbornness and did what God wanted. In the parable neither son is praiseworthy; but of the two, the one who eventually obeys receives the praise.

The parable is in harmony with Jesus' words in the Sermon on the Mount. "Blessed are the poor in spirit," those who have nothing to offer God except their humility; "blessed are the meek," those who in their humility are ready to offer everything to God (their weaknesses and their strengths) for His purposes.

Having no pride in a righteousness of their own, they allow God's love to forgive them and His goals for their lives to become their goals, too. Like most new converts who come to Christ from a life of disappointing sinfulness, they are eager to obey, aware of their dependency upon God, hungry to learn more spiritual truths.

It is that readiness to obey that Jesus commends.

We are ready, then, for the second question: *Can one really believe in God and not obey Him?*

Jesus answers this question in verse 32. "For John came to you in the way of righteousness, and you did not *believe* him, but the tax collectors and the harlots *believed* him; and even when you saw it, you did not afterward *repent* and *believe* him."

When the sinners believed John the Baptist, they wanted to please him and God. That desire led them to repent of their past rebellion against God and to accept John's baptism as a sign of their obedience. Within the parable, Jesus alludes to their change of heart (which is what repentance means) by saying that the son *"repented* and went."

The sequence of events on the Day of Pentecost (Acts 2:36-42) illustrates this natural tie between belief and obedience. At the conclusion of Peter's sermon, the consience-stricken people cried out to know what to do; and Peter exhorted them to repent and to be baptized. The people obviously believed the word of the Lord as Peter preached it. They knew themselves guilty of heinuous sins against Christ. Like the son in the parable, they repented of their disobedience to God, and they evidenced their repentance by submitting to baptism. Their new obedience did not stop there, either. They then "devoted themselves to the apostles' teaching and fellowship, to the breaking of bread and the prayers." The Acts record continues with its testimony to their continuing obedience to the Lord.

In spite of their claims of belief in God, then, the chief priests and elders stand condemned by Christ as disobedient to the will of God because, after hearing the message of John, they did not repent and obey.

To believe is to obey.

A Communist cannot say "I am a disciple of Marx and Lenin and a faithful member of the Communist party" if he is consistently disobedient to the teachings of Marx and Lenin.

In World War II when a man said "I am a Nazi" the world shuddered, because he meant that he believed in Adolf Hitler and *would be obedient* to him to death.

Then can one say, "I believe in Jesus Christ" and ignore or disobey His commands? He said, "If you love me, you will keep my commandments" (John 14:15).

When Peter and the apostles heard the high priest forbid them to speak about Jeus any more, they could only reply, "We must obey God rather than men." Faith in God could do no less (Acts 5:29).

It is faith, the apostle Paul says in Philippians 3:9, that leads to righteousness.

"By *faith* Abraham *obeyed* when he was called to go out to a place which he was to receive as an inheritance; and he went out, not knowing where he was to go" (Hebrews 11:8).

Is it any wonder to us, after looking at these Scriptures, that Jesus can equate the *obedience* of the son in the parable with the *belief* and *repentance* of the tax collectors and prostitutes?

Since this truth seems clear, we must ask our next question: *Why does the second son lie rather than obey?*

"Lie" may seem too strong a word. But is it? Does he in fact intend to do his father's will? The parable doesn't say.

Perhaps he intends to obey, but is just a bit irresponsible. But when one's word cannot be trusted, when he cannot be counted on to do what he says, isn't he in effect the same as a liar?

Jesus does not call him a liar, so we should not either. Maybe he is just undisciplined, really desiring to please his father but unable to apply himself to the task.

Perhaps he is just distracted by his many other interests.

Or is he like many persons who entertain lovely religious feelings and who therefore substitute right feelings for right actions? It is not unusual for one to be moved in the presence of God to utter a virtuous wish or to resolve to do some generous deed, without even guessing that he will be unable to follow through.

Is he too busy? Is his schedule already so crammed that he doesn't have time to do anything unscheduled for his father?

Perhaps he is on his way to the work when a friend comes along and lures him away.

Or is it possible that, fully intending to go, he bogs down in his preparations—waterproofing his boots, sharpening his plow, rebuilding the trough, eating his meals—so that his elaborate preparations make it impossible for him to get to the field? In the same way, preoccupation with the preparation for worship and service can sometimes take the place of service itself.

Probably he is just a creature of habit, who simply lets "doin' what comes natur'ly" keep him from fulfilling his father's wishes.

Whatever the reason, or excuse, the father is disappointed and the son is disobedient, in spite of his polite "I go, sir."

The other son's change of behavior raises the final question: *Why does he repent?* His first answer to his father's request, churlish and disrespectful, is bad enough. It does, however, possess the virtue of honesty, which is more than can be said for his brother's response. But why does he change?

Obviously he respects his father, in spite of his language. He seems like many apparently hardened cases today. They "won't be found dead" in a church building. They do everything they know the church is against. Their behavior is hardly commendable—yet they have not lost respect for God, and they harbor a secret desire to please Him.

Can it be that the rebellious son has grown disgusted with himself? Sin sometimes brings its own conviction, especially to those who know better. "There has to be something better for life," they realize. "I'm better than this, I've been taught better than this. My father has given me higher standards."

Now We Understand

Whatever the reason, the son repents. To repent, by the way, does not mean a change of heart or mind only, but a change that leads to action. His repentance is genuine, we know, because he now does what his father wants. He does not content himself with simply feeling sorry that he has offended his father. That's not repentance. His sorrow moves him and he does his father's will. Is this "godly sorrow"? See 2 Corinthians 7:9, 10.

Now we understand why harlots and tax collectors may precede chief priests and elders into the kingdom. It is not because of their sinfulness, nor because of their new self-made righteousness, or "because they really want to do the will of God."

Now they believe.

They repent.

They obey.

They know that to believe is to obey.

10

The Perils of the Head Table

Luke 14:1, 7-11

These verses do not read like a parable. There is no extended narrative, only a brief warning. The second person *you* is used instead of the usual third person *he*.

The parable is not so much in Jesus' words as in what is happening in front of Him. Jesus is just supplying the commentary. Some of the important men among the guests are making their way, probably quite without thinking, to the honored seats at the head table. Others, esteeming themselves to be of less worth, find less conspicuous places.

Nothing extraordinary is happening. At any formal feast, the host is careful to honor his guests according to their rank or social prominence. And not infrequently some in the crowd think of themselves more highly than they ought and push themselves forward to claim some of the chief seats. We have no trouble imagining just such a person, overweight and pompous and convinced that in occupying an honored place he is simply receiving his due. We cannot help smiling as we picture the exasperated host tapping him on the shoulder, whispering that he has taken the seat meant for another, asking the usurper to move to a lower place. We become embarrassed for him as we watch him, red-faced, making his way to the only place left, at the foot of the table.

Thus, Jesus says, are the mighty humbled.

To avoid this involuntary humbling, Jesus urges His audience to adopt the virtue of genuine humility. He is not speaking of something they have not already been taught.

> Do not put yourself forward in the king's presence
>   or stand in the place of the great;
> for it is better to be told, "Come up here,"
>   than to be put lower in the presence of the prince
>   (Proverbs 25:6, 7).

In spite of all such proverbs and exhortations to practice humility, however, and regardless of the nearly universal praise of humble persons, no Christian virtue is more neglected than this one. Who does not desire to sit at the head table?

Jesus undoubtedly catches His fellow guests off guard with His teaching. At first they think He is giving them a lesson in etiquette. When He reaches the moral (verse 11), however, they know that He is calling their attention to a spiritual principle that governs life even in the very practical matter of seat selection at a banquet.

The "Spiritual" in the "Practical"

Throughout the parables Jesus teaches—for those who have ears to hear—that the Christian life should not be thought to be "impractical" or "otherworldly." Spiritual life is not confined to praying, Bible reading, and Sunday worship. It governs the spending of money, management of households, forgiveness of debtors, healing the sick, clothing the naked, feeding the hungry. It even dictates where one sits at a table!

By simply selecting the chief seats, some men in Jesus' sight betrayed their captivity to the deadliest enemy to a rich spiritual life: pride.

Pride is attacked throughout the Bible and even on the pages written by the world's wisest philosophers. "For God abases the proud, but he saves the lowly," Eliphaz the Temanite reminds Job (Job 22:29). "Blessed are the meek, for they shall inherit the earth" is Jesus' promise to those who have conquered their pride (Matthew 5:5). The wise pagan philosopher Epictetus discovered the same thing:

> What is the first business of one who studies philosophy? To part with self-conceit. For it is impossible for anyone to begin to learn what he thinks that he already knows.

As we read these words we nod in agreement; then we leave our studies and contradict ourselves, walking proudly before man and God. The Pharisee who happened to be at prayer with the publican (Luke 18:9-14) knew very well that God is on the side of the humble. Although his arrogance is transparent to us, he undoubtedly was not aware of it. After all, he proved his humility before God to himself by his fasting, tithing, and correct living. He saw no self-contradiction.

Perhaps the Pharisee's problem was that he was just too "religious," concentrating too exclusively on the rules of his religion, the requirements of his God, so that he hadn't noticed a sense of self-satisfaction creeping in. He had devoted himself to mastering the demands of his faith. He knew—such things are obvious—that he lived more uprightly than others, especially the tax collector. He had played the game of religion according to the prescribed rules, and he had become an expert at it. He expected others to defer to him on religious questions and would have been offended, perhaps, if he had not been given one of the best seats.

With Jesus at the banquet were other men like this Pharisee. They were quite satisfied with their position on spiritual issues, but they were unaware that their arrogance at the table was an affront to God. So Jesus talked about their etiquette, and in so doing He erased the line between "the practical" and "the spiritual." Where we sit at the table, how we crowd into a line ahead of others, how we display status symbols to prove our superiority—in these and countless other practical matters we betray our real spiritual values. We may even show them to people around us when we are not aware of them ourselves.

The Problem of Pride

The problem of pride is the specific issue here. The ancient Greeks called it *hubris* and pinned this label upon any person who usurped the prerogatives of the gods. It is the theme of the Greek tragedies: Why can men not be content to be men? Why do they ruinously aspire to behave as gods?

Observers of our Washington scene during the Watergate days saw a Greek tragedy performed before them, when powerful men lost everything because of their *hubris*. We do not call it *hubris*, of course, but borrow President Wilson's term for it, *Potomac Fever*. According to President Truman, Wilson said that "some people came to Washington and grew with their jobs, but . . . a lot of other people came, and all they did was swell up." Those that swell up are the ones that have Potomac Fever. Truman adds that they are the people who forget who they are and who sent them there.[1]

That is precisely the problem with pride. It causes us to forget who we are and who sent us here. No conscientious Christian, aware of his sins and thankful for the grace of God who has forgiven those sins and given new life, should be able quickly to forget who he is. But some seem to forget—and all are tempted to. Perhaps the Russian novelist Dostoevsky, commenting upon the French, of whom he was never fond, says something about some of us as well:

> It is impossible to undeceive a Frenchman and prevent his believing himself the most important being in the wide world. Besides, of the wide world he is pretty ignorant. And what is more, he is not keen to be enlightened.[2]

What an indictment! He knows not and knows not that he knows not, but knows that he does not want to know. That's the problem with pride—it is ignorant and does not want to be reminded.

How to Be Humble

In the face of this universal problem of pride, how shall we assume humility? *The meaning of humility is simpler to understand than its practice is to achieve.* Its importance is such that Augustine, the great early church father, wrote, "Should you ask me, What is the first thing in religion? I should reply, 'The first, second, and third thing therein—nay, all—is humility.' "[3]

The humble remember who they are. They know themselves to be children of God, servants of His will. As adopted sons and daughters of the Almighty, they need not bow down before anyone on earth; but as princes and princesses of the King, they refuse to flaunt their royalty before anyone or contest the demands of others to go first. They know who they are; they do not need to prove themselves to anyone else. Their humility rests securely in their knowledge of God's love for them.

In *Zorba the Greek,* Kazantzakis tells the delightful fable of a crow who used to walk quite respectably until one day he determined to strut like a pigeon. He worked so hard at it that from that day on the poor fellow couldn't remember his own way of walking. He just hobbled about most absurdly. He forgot who he was!

A Christian knows himself to be more "crow" than "pigeon." He wants to serve God rather than parade before man.

The humble remember whom they serve. "Serve" is the important word. Jesus had to remind His disciples that "whoever would be great among you must be your servant, and whoever would be first among you must be your slave." Even the Son of man, he explained, "came not to be served but to serve" (Matthew 20:26-28).

Nowhere does Jesus promise His disciples a place at the head tables of this earth. He assigns them the tasks of foot-washing, wine-serving, message-carrying, and finally cross-bearing.

In an incident from the midst of the civil war, that American embodiment of humility, President Lincoln, illustrates Jesus' instructions. He had to suffer the arrogance of hesitant, ineffectual General McClellan, chief of all the Republic's armies. The General had such low regard for the president that he regularly snubbed him. Once, when Lincoln came to his headquarters for a conference, McClellan even went to bed, an unpardonable affront. "Never mind," said Lincoln, "I will hold McClellan's horse if he will only bring us success."[4]

Lincoln has become a symbol of humility to Americans because of his ability to remember, even when ridiculed and insulted, whom he served. He had a nation to serve.

The humble give God the glory. That's the Christian's goal. They do not aspire to be in the spotlight. They do their work. If it earns praise, let the praise be to God, whom they serve. They know there is great ability in knowing how to conceal ability. If they boast, they boast like the poet John Donne:

> I have done one braver thing
> Than all the worthies did,
> And yet a braver thence doth spring,
> Which is, to keep that hid.

They have heeded the words of Paul: "So, whether you eat or drink, or whatever you do, do all to the glory of God" (1 Corinthians 10:31).

The humble have learned to like the lowest seats. They have grown accustomed to putting others first, to applauding the stars in the performance, to giving honor to whom honor is due. They don't mind straining to hear, craning their necks to see. They squirm uncomfortably when made the center of attention.

They may, in fact, have adjusted so comfortably to the humbler position that they will resist being moved to the head table even when requested. But in their humility they go, even against their will, so long as they are convinced it is the Master's will. Only then.

The humble want to be like Jesus.

> Have this mind among yourselves, which you have in Christ Jesus, who, though he was in the form of God, did not count equality with God a thing to be grasped, but emptied himself, taking the form of a servant, being born in the likeness of men. And being found in human form he humbled himself and became obedient unto death, even death on a cross. Therefore God has highly exalted him . . . (Philippians 2:5-9).

Notes

1. Merle Miller, *Plain Speaking.* New York: Berkley Publishing, © 1973, 1974, p. 150.

2. *Dostoevsky* by André Gide. Copyright © 1961 by New Directions Publishing Corporation. Reprinted by permission of New Directions Publishing Corporation.

3. Harold A. Boxley, Ph.D., *He Spoke to Them in Parables.* New York, Evanston, and London: Harper and Row Publishers, © 1963.

4. Samuel Morrison, *The Oxford History of the American People.* New York: Oxford University Press, 1965, p. 636.

11

Foolish Success

Luke 12:13-21

"Teacher, make my brother give me everything that's coming to me!"

"I want my share!"

How familiar these words are! Ask any lawyer or counselor in an inheritance dispute, and he will tell you scores of stories about disputed wills, one relative of the deceased suing another because of supposed inequities in the will or improper executing of the will's provisions. Each claimant wants "everything that's coming to me!"

Of course some people demand more than they ought to have. It is hard to be just when our own wealth is involved. But we may betray our greed even when we ask no more than justice.

Jesus' petitioner may have justice on his side. Perhaps his brother has actually cheated him out of his just portion. If so, he naturally turns to Jesus to settle his dispute, as Jews often turn to their rabbis.

He is surely disappointed in Jesus' answer. The Teacher treats the problem lightly. "What difference does this little inequity make?" Jesus seems to be asking. "You have a much deeper problem. You suffer from *pleonexia,* covetousness. Its more common name is greed."

Or foolishness. Its source is the mistaken notion that man's life consists in the abundance of possessions. This mistake leads to a greedy desire to have more—more of what does not really matter.

To help the petitioner see himself, Jesus tells him the story of a successful but foolish businessman. Agriculture is his business. He's no poor dirt farmer, but a thriving, shrewd, respectable landowner.

Among his peers, he undoubtedly is accorded honors. At least in our country men would praise him for his success.

Jesus, on the other hand, calls him a fool.

In this brief story our cherished values slam against the immovable truth that God's ways are not our ways, that God has made foolish the wisdom of the world (1 Corinthians 1:20).

What Is Done

We would call the farmer *successful.* The reasons for doing so are obvious.

He takes care of his *crops*, Jesus says. He purchases the best seed, plants in carefully cultivated fields, harvests at the height of the grain's maturity. Of course he has help from the weather—but there is no indication that he gives the climate any credit for his bumper crop.

He takes care of his *property.* When his harvest returns a profit, he thinks carefully about investing it. He does not squander or gamble it away. He undoubtedly has adequate insurance coverage and diversifies his holdings in stocks and bonds, with a cushion against any adversity tucked away in savings certificates earning the highest available interest.

He also has provided for his *comfort.* He is no miser, hoarding his precious earnings but not enjoying them.

To the contrary, he does not deny himself the luxuries of life. "Finally," he says to himself, "the hard work of my younger days has paid off. Now I can take it easy. I've earned the right! No one has worked harder than I, nor sacrificed more. It is time to cash in on my years of hard labor."

Many adopt ease and happiness as ends in themselves. An idealist like Albert Einstein may accuse them of holding "the ideal of a pigsty,"[1] but most of us would heartily approve of the farmer's motives as normal and wish we were in a position to do likewise.

We too would take care of our *pleasures.* We would "eat, drink, and be merry" with him. We would perhaps be no more aware of how selfish we would sound than the farmer is of the self-centeredness in his words. They sound somewhat like the song of the little girl:

> I gave a little party this afternoon at three;
> 'Twas very small, three guests in all, just
>   I, myself and me.
> Myself ate all the sandwiches, while I drank
>   up the tea,
> And it was I who ate the pie, and passed the
>   cake to me.

The farmer would receive praise primarily, however, because he so effectively prepares for his *future security.* He invests in his future. Although Jesus reprimands His disciples for their anxiety about tomorrow (see the following verses), most of us work daily with one eye on retirement. "What are your retirement benefits?" we ask any prospective employer. "Do you have adequate health and accident insurance, do you pay social security, what are your fringe benefits?" All these questions melt into one: "Is my future secure?"

The farmer thinks his is.

That's why God calls him a fool.

What Is Undone

Although he takes care of his crops, his property, his comfort, his pleasures, and his future security, he leaves too much undone. There is no indication that he thinks about giving anything away. Apparently he does not know the truth of Jesus' statement, "Whoever seeks to gain his life will lose it, but whoever loses his life will preserve it" (Luke 17:33).

Nor does he know that a man who says only "I" lives in mortal danger. In this brief parable, the farmer uses "I" or "my" eleven times. Not once does he say "we" or "our."

Not only is his life in mortal danger, but he is dangerous to those around him. He invites theft, even revolution, by living so luxuriously while others, in spite of their hard work, struggle to exist.

He is a fool, then, because of what he does not take care of.

He does not mention his family. He undoubtedly would protest to any critic that he has really provided for them. But he does not mention them here. They are obviously not his first concern. Even if he has given them every material luxury, his spiritual poverty has impoverished them. As the spiritual head of his house, he is a failure.

What, for example, will his children inherit from him? Houses and barns and Cadillacs only? What will they have when their father's money runs out? Will they have character resources to replenish their loss? Will he have given them any of those important things that money cannot buy? The final problem for any loving father is not how he will provide for his retirement, but how his heirs are going to live. To ask that question is to wonder what kind of persons children of such a selfish father can become. He has failed to take care of their personal welfare.

The rich man says not a word about his neighbors. In his success he has forgotten that neighbors need each other. He undoubtedly needed them when, as a young man, he barely eked out a living on his small plot of land. Now, in his prosperity, they need him: his advice, his tools, his friendship, and perhaps his money.

The parable of the good Samaritan (Luke 10:29-37) does not allow us to define neighbor only as the one who lives next door, either. While the rich farmer prepares to indulge his expensive tastes in food and drink, he ignores the teeming masses of his world who are groveling for half-a-handful of grain to quiet their aching stomachs.

Twentieth-century Americans, who eat at a banquet table three times a day, have hungry neighbors. Headlong we hustle to produce more and more money to provide larger and larger banquets for ourselves while starving millions watch us with hunger-weakened eyes. Does this invite God's judgment of fool?

The farmer has not taken care of his obligation to God, either. He does not pray; he thinks to himself. He shows no awareness of God's sovereignty over life and death. Perhaps he thinks he grew his crops alone, without any help from God's creating and sustaining power.

If he prays at all, his prayers must sound something like "My soul, which art on earth, hallowed be my name. My kingdom come; my will be done on earth as it is in my mind. Give me this day my daily bread . . ."

Where's God in this story?

For that matter, where's the man? Has he really taken care of his soul?

William Barclay records the story of a conversation between a young and ambitious lad and one older and wiser.[2]

> "I will," said the young man, "learn my trade."
> "And then?" asked his more experienced friend.
> "I will set up in business."
> "And then?"
> "I will make my fortune."
> "And then?"

"I suppose I shall grow old and retire and live on my money."

"And then?"

"Well, I suppose some day I will die."

"And then?"

Now it is obvious why God calls the rich farmer a fool. The one thing he is most certain he has provided for—his security—he has most certainly neglected. He has stopped one "and then" too soon.

He has forgotten Job 27:8: "For what is the hope of the godless when God cuts him off, when God takes away his life?"

What Needs to Be Done

What then, should the rich farmer have done?

More specifically, what shall we do? The answer is suggested in 1 Timothy 6:6-10.

There is great gain in godliness with contentment; for we brought nothing into the world, and we cannot take anything out of the world; but if we have food and clothing, with these we shall be content. But those who desire to be rich fall into temptation, into a snare, into many senseless and hurtful desires that plunge men into ruin and destruction. For the love of money is the root of all evils; it is through this craving that some have wandered away from the faith and pierced their hearts with many pangs.

It is also found in Matthew 6:25-33.

Therefore I tell you, do not be anxious about your life, what you shall eat or what you shall drink, nor about your body, what you shall put on. Is not life more than food, and the body more than clothing? Look at the birds of the air: they neither sow nor reap nor gather into barns, and yet your heavenly Father feeds them. Are you not of more value than they? And which of you by being anxious can add one cubit to his span of life? And why are you anxious about clothing? Consider the lilies of the field, how they grow; they neither toil nor spin; yet I tell you, even Solomon in all his glory was not arrayed like one of these. But if God so clothes the grass of the field, which today is alive and tomorrow is thrown into the oven, will he not much more clothe you, O men of little faith? Therefore do not be anxious, saying, "What shall we eat?" or "What shall we drink?" or "What shall we wear?" For the Gentiles seek all these things; and your heavenly Father knows that you need them all. But seek first his kingdom and his righteousness, and all these things shall be yours as well.

Then let us lay not up treasure for ourselves, but be rich toward God!

Notes

1. Taken from *Ideas and Opinions* by Albert Einstein. Copyright © 1954 by Crown Publishers, Inc. Used by permission of Crown Publishers, Inc.

2. The Daily Study Bible: *The Gospel of Luke.* Philadelphia: The Westminster Press, 1956, pp. 168-169.

12

How Often Shall I Forgive?

Matthew 18:21-35

When President John Kennedy was shot to death by Lee Harvey Oswald on November 22, 1963, a stunned nation turned to God for help. Lyndon Johnson accepted the mantle of the presidency, asking his countrymen to pray for him. Sermons and prayers were offered for him and for the Kennedy family from practically every pulpit in the land.

Of course not all the praying was done in church. Parents and children knelt together in hundreds of homes. Prayers were offered in PTA meetings, in women's clubs, in luncheon clubs where prayers were seldom heard except when the chaplain said grace before lunch. Even in schools there were prayers.

Did anyone pray for Oswald?

The assassin was immediately caught and imprisoned. When he was shot by Jack Ruby three days later the nation was shocked, but not sorry that he was gone.

One woman, however, grieved for him. On the day after his death, this new Christian whose own life had been scarred by personal tragedies handed her minister a poem. In it she voiced Oswald's imagined plea for forgiveness, the forgiveness she had experienced when she brought her guilt-tormented life to Christ.

Ah, but I too am dead.
Oh, people of this favored land,
Think once of me.
Mine is a cold and barren grave:
Dishonor sleeps alone.
Because I was unknown, unloved,
The more I need your tears.
Whatever scheme
Or plan
Or fate
Drove me to this—this act
That took this bless'd and burdened man
  From country and from life,
No matter what the cause, or lack of cause,
Or reason, or its lack—
Oh God, I cry, hear Thou my pleas,
Let Thy wronged and grieving people
Weep a prayer for me.

When the minister read the lines, he was profoundly moved by her compassion, her readiness to forgive. As a new Christian, she more readily knew that God's desire to forgive must be matched by the willingness of His people to do the same, even in extreme circumstances.

It is a lesson we should not need, because we could nor survive without being forgiven for so much.

As a husband, I am held to my wife by her forgiveness.

As a father, I am held to my children by their forgiveness.

As a friend, I am held to my friend by his forgiveness.

As a Christian, I am held to my Lord by His forgiveness.

Forgiveness says, "Our relationship is more important than any offense you have committed against me."

That is why Jesus answers Peter's troubled question as He does. "Peter, you must forgive and forgive and forgive in order to keep ahold of your brother." "Seventy times seven" is not a mathematical formula, but an indication of the lengths to which God has gone in forgiving us and to which we must now go in forgiving each other.

God's Mercy and Ours

The forgiveness of God is almost without limit, according to this parable. The king, who obviously represents God, forgives his debtor an enormous amount; according to the Revised Standard Version, approximately ten million dollars, before inflation! No one to whom Jesus is speaking can even comprehend such a fortune. There is no way the debtor can repay the debt. That, of course, is precisely Jesus' point. The debtor has no recourse other than to throw himself upon the mercy of the king, who forgives the debt.

When the released servant confronts his own debtor, who owes him an amount five or six hundred thousand times smaller, he demands full payment and shows no mercy.

The king acts with the mercy of God, his servant with the mercilessness that characterizes most human transactions. Divine mercy keeps no score; it does not count to seven, or even to seventy times seven. Peter, you must forsake your human arithmetic, your human demands for strict justice, and place yourself in the shoes of the one who has sinned against you, because you have sinned more grievously against God.

God has forgiven not only our sins, by the way, but also our feeble attempts at righteousness. He hears us alike when we pray with the publican, "God, be merciful to me a sinner!" and when, surveying our most conscientious efforts to live a Christian life, we still pray, in the words penned by the poet Wordsworth many years ago:[1]

The best of what we do and are,
Just God, forgive.
How thankful we are that
There's a wideness in God's mercy,
Like the wideness of the sea,
There's a kindness in His justice,
Which is more than liberty.
For the love of God is broader
Than the measure of man's mind;
And the heart of the eternal
Is most wonderfully kind.

There is a limit to His mercy, however. *The forgiveness of God is limited—by ours.* Just as Jesus couples the love of God with the love of neighbor (Mark 12:28-31), so He makes our continued enjoyment of God's forgiveness conditional upon our mercy towards those who have offended us.

In the Sermon on the Mount Jesus summarizes the teaching of this parable:

Blessed are the merciful, for they shall obtain mercy (Matthew 5:7).

And forgive us our debts, as we also have forgiven our debtors (Matthew 6:12).

For if you forgive men their trespasses, your heavenly Father also will forgive you; but if you do not forgive men their trespasses, neither will your Father forgive your trespasses (Matthew 6:14, 15).

The apostle Paul, concerned about internal harmony in the lives of the churches, constantly returns in his letters to the theme of forgiving. The basis for his appeal is consistently the fact that Christ has forgiven us:

Let all bitterness and wrath and anger and clamor and slander be put away from you, with all malice, and be kind to one another, tenderhearted, *forgiving* one another, as God in Christ *forgave* you (Ephesians 4:31).

> Put on then, as God's chosen ones, holy and beloved, compassion, kindness, lowliness, meekness, and patience, forbearing one another and, if one has a complaint against another, *forgiving* each other; as the Lord has *forgiven* you, so you also must *forgive* (Colossians 3:12, 13).

In the second Corinthian letter, Paul adds another reason. By forgiving each other, we handicap Satan in his assaults on us.

> What I have forgiven, if I have forgiven anything, has been for your sake in the presence of Christ, *to keep Satan from gaining the advantage* over us; for we are not ignorant of his designs (2 Corinthians 2:10, 11).

Danger!

An unforgiving person is in mortal danger. Having once tasted the freedom and joy of standing before God and man without guilt, like the first debtor in the parable, he can quickly arouse the wrath of God through his callous treatment of his fellow sinner. The love of God cannot tolerate one of His children's deliberate abuse of another.

It is apparent that the consequences of such a hardness of heart do not await a final judgment, either. Any physician or minister can tell far too many stories of men and women being treated for diverse symptoms from which they cannot be cured, because their real disease is an unforgiving heart. Their bitterness has poisoned them. Their illness may be fatal. If only they could show mercy, then they could be saved!

An unforgiving world is in equal danger. The parable has implications for world peace and order, doesn't it? How many wars could have been avoided, how many human lives saved, had national leaders sought to show mercy rather than revenge! How can there ever be peace when governments are led by violent, vindictive men?

The July 1960 *Reader's Digest* quoted then Premier Nikita Khrushchev of the Soviet Union on a visit to Rouen Cathedral. He said that Communists and Christ have much in common, but then added,

> But I cannot agree with Him when he says when you are hit on the right cheek turn the left cheek. I believe in another principle. If I am hit on the left cheek I hit back on the right cheek so hard the head might fall off.

"That," he said, "is my sole difference with Christ."[2]

That is the difference, however, that has kept our planet embroiled in wars throughout human history.

Perhaps Jesus' teaching makes sense after all. Since there is no other path to peace than that of mercy and forgiveness, Jesus' disciples must begin to take His words seriously—and forgive.

Nothing in the parable indicates that forgiveness is easy, of course—just that it is required.

Demonstration

At the close of His earthly ministry, *Jesus demonstrates what forgiveness means.* The supreme demonstration is the cross, certainly. But in another very personal way He shows Peter what it is all about.

When the women come to the tomb on resurrection morning, they are greeted by the angel of God who announces that Jesus is not there, for He has been raised from the dead. According to the account in Mark's Gospel, the angel then instructs the women to "go, tell his disciples and Peter that he is going before you to Galilee . . ."

At first glance, it seems strange that the angel does not single out the beloved disciple, John, or even Thomas, the doubter. Peter alone is mentioned by name. The angel specifies Peter for a very simple reason. Peter was the one who needed special mention.

Just a short time earlier, in the severest crisis of Jesus' ministry, when He needed His friends the most, Peter cursed and lied and denied that he ever knew Him.

What great guilt is his! What awful sorrow!

How can he face God any more? How can he even face his friends, before whom he has flatly denied that he will ever desert the Lord?

Because his guilt is so great, and God's mercy so generous, the angel sends the women to tell Peter. He will know, then, that he is forgiven. The long arm of the love of God can reach beyond his denial.

". . . as the Lord has forgiven you . . ."

Notes
1. "Memorials of a Tour In Scotland."
2. *Reader's Digest,* July 1960, p. 136.

13

The Final Separation
Matthew 13:24-30, 36-43, 47-50

In the popular Christian imagination, no subject arises more frequently than that of judgment and damnation. Pictures of boiling cauldrons stirred by grinning fiends, of naked bodies writhing in ecstasies of torture—these dominate our artists' attempts to capture the awfulness of hell. Earlier preachers like the nineteenth-century Charles H. Spurgeon promise that hell will be like this gruesome picture:

> There is a real fire in hell, as truly as you have a real body—a fire exactly like that which we have on this earth, except this: that it will not consume, though it will torture you. You have seen asbestos lying amid red hot coals, but not consumed. So your body will be prepared by God in such a way that it will burn forever without being consumed. With your nerves laid raw by the searing flame, yet never desensitized for all its raging fury, and the acrid smoke of the sulphurous fumes searing your lungs and choking your breath, you will cry out for the mercy of death, but it shall never, never, *no never* give you surcease.[1]

Such, says Spurgeon, is the judgment to come for those who are not God's elect.

The Pictures Jesus Gives

The two parables we are considering in this chapter are also pictures of judgment. Jesus uses less vivid language than Spurgeon, and He does not dwell on the nature of the punishment for the lost, but He does predict a judgment that will separate wheat from weeds, edible fish from junk fish.

There will be a harvest, Jesus promises. In His teachings, Jesus never loses sight of the fact that God is in charge of all history and is working toward His goals. Just as time began when God spoke the world into being, so the age will close when His goals have been accomplished.

The Son of man then is God's agent, working to insure a large harvest of men and women when God sends His reapers into the field. The field, Jesus teaches, is the world. We cannot read these words without recalling the Great Commission (Matthew 28:18-20) and Jesus' instructions to His disciples in Acts 1:8 that they would witness to Him to the end of the earth. The worldwide missionary enterprise of the church continues Christ's sowing work, planting "sons of the kingdom" on every continent to produce a full harvest.

But the Son of man is not the only one sowing. The enemy—the sneaky, trespassing, malicious, trouble-making devil—is also planting his own kind of seeds, growing his crop of antagonists. *Sneaky* is not a bad word to describe him, since he plants bearded darnel, a plant resembling wheat so closely in the early stages of its growth that it is impossible to distinguish between them.

Jesus does not accuse the devil of placing the poisonous or inedible fish among the good fish in the net; but as anyone who has fished with a large net knows, the net will trap all kinds of sea animals, many of which will have to be rejected.

To speak of a harvest of wheat and fish, then, is to speak of a judgment. The wheat (and good fish) will go into the keeping of the Son of man; the weeds (and the bad fish) will be gathered and cast away.

We should remember that the "furnace of fire" is only one of the New Testament pictures of destiny awaiting the sons of the evil one. Here are some others:

> "eternal punishment" (Matthew 25:46)
> "eternal destruction and exclusion from the presence of the Lord" (2 Thessalonians 1:9)
> "destruction" (Philippians 1:28)
> "wrath and fury . . . tribulation and distress" (Romans 2:8, 9)
> "hell, where their worm does not die, and the fire is not quenched" (Mark 9:47, 48)
> "the lake of fire" (Revelation 20:14, 15)

Biblical language about the sentences of God's judgment upon the lost is strong. Its purpose is not to provide a literal picture of the damned so much as to convince us of how terrible life apart from the presence of God would be. We do an injustice to the Bible and to these parables if we concentrate more on the fate of the weeds than we do on the prospects of the wheat. We do well to heed the warning of C. S. Lewis:

> There are two equal and opposite errors into which our race can fall about the devils. One is to disbelieve in their existence. The other is to believe and then feel an excessive and unhealthy interest in them.[2]

What he says of devils is equally true of the abode of the devils. After all, as the late Jesse Bader used to say of the evangelistic program of the church, our task is to "get folks into the kingdom and then get the kingdom into folks." To accomplish that purpose, we must pay more heed to the Son of man and His sowing than to the devil and his.

The Judge and Savior

There will be a judgment—and the Son of man will make the decisions.

He has to. Bearded darnel is slightly poisonous; it must be removed from the wheat.

He has to. Not all fish are good.

He has to. Only He knows the hearts of men. Evil is no mystery to Him, nor are the burdens of men. In early stages of growth, wheat and tares (sons of the kingdom and the sons of the evil one) look alike. But when the harvest comes, the reapers (instructed by the Son of man) can tell the difference.

George Bernard Shaw, that cynical but honest Irish author of *Man and Superman,* says through Don Juan in that play, "Hell is the home of honor, duty, justice, and the rest of the seven deadly virtues. All the wickedness on earth is done in their name." But, we protest, aren't we bound in Christ's name to be honorable, dutiful, and just? Of course. But isn't Shaw correct in reminding us that no evil against humanity has been perpetrated in the name of evil, but in the name of honor, duty, justice, national security, purifying the race, etc.? Obviously, human intelligence has grave difficulty in separating wheat from tares! No wonder Jesus warned us against judging (Matthew 7:1-5).

While it is correct to think of the Son of man as judge, it is with some reservation that Jesus applies the title to himself. In John 12:47, 48, He denies that He does the judging:

> If any one hears my sayings and does not keep them, I do not judge him; for I did not come to judge the world but to save the world. He who rejects me and does not receive

92

my sayings has a judge; the word that I have spoken will be his judge on the last day.

To think of Christ primarily as judge is to distort His ministry among mankind. His earthly purpose, as His name indicates (Matthew 1:21), is to be the Savior of His people. Furthermore, even in His capacity as final judge He does not arbitrarily select some for salvation and others for condemnation. Those who stand before Him have already decided their fate. He has spoken the word of truth to them. How they have responded to that word has sealed their future.

Our future, then, is in our own hands. "He who rejects me," says Jesus, "rejects him who sent me" (Luke 10:16). How can one who rejects God be considered a son of His kingdom?

The Imperfect Kingdom

In both these parables Jesus assures His followers that *the kingdom will not be pure before the close of the age.* (His words remind one of the cartoon in *Look* magazine several years ago. One worried minister is saying to his brother of the cloth, "Oh, I know what the world is coming to eventually. I just wonder what it's coming to in the meantime.") The householder's servants want to pluck out the weeds to purify the crop. To do so, however, might damage the good wheat. Both wheat and weeds therefore will be allowed to grow together until the harvest, just as both good and bad fish are pulled ashore by the dragnet. There will be time later for separating.

Verse 41 makes clear that the good and bad live side by side not only in the world but also in the kingdom prior to judgment: "They will gather *out of his kingdom* all causes of sin and all evildoers." The message of the parable is clear; God is letting wheat and tares grow together for now. His angels will separate them at the proper time.

The message to the church is equally clear; to strive too vigorously to preserve a pure church is to risk plucking out the good along with the bad. The implications for church discipline, then, must be explored. Is it possible to maintain absolute doctrinal purity in a church? Or for that matter, how does a congregation guarantee moral purity among the members? The apostle Paul begs his readers of the Ephesian letter "to lead a life worthy of the calling" to which they have been called (Ephesians 4:1). He tells the Cointhians that a deliberate and persistent sinner must be excluded from the fellowship of Christians (1 Corinthians 5:1, 2). From Paul's day to the present, conscientious church leaders have struggled to know what to do with members who apparently violate the high standards of Christian behavior.

The result of this high-principled concern has often been what some students of the church call "ghetto religion," with the church separated and aloof from the world, excluding all who do not evidence the piety that is considered proper. Critics of such churches call their members self-righteous and compare them with the Pharisees who condemned Jesus for His easy association with tax collectors and sinners. Defenders of these churches congratulate the members for keeping themselves pure and unspotted by the world.

Jesus seems to tolerate imperfection in the kingdom on earth. In these parables He admits the real difference between the sons of the kingdom and the sons of the evil one, but resists His disciples' temptation to separate them before the harvest. The sons of the kingdom will dwell with the rest of humanity.

A cursory reading of the book of Acts proves that *the early church followed Jesus' instructions*. On the Day of Pentecost, three thousand were added to the church. Peter's invitation to his audience to "save yourselves from this crooked generation" opened its doors. No entrance test was required of the respondents to guarantee that only the pure were received into membership. The requirements were faith, repentance, and baptism. Although a spotless life was held before the members as the goal for Christian growth, perfection was not required for membership. The result was a membership almost as varied as humanity itself, with all human problems challenging the leaders—and undoubtedly frequently tempting them to tear out the weeds!

Now Hear This

To modern readers of the parables, Christ's instruction here is the same as to those who first heard Him: "He who has ears, let him hear."

Let him hear—that there will be judgment, a separation, between the sons of the kingdom and the sons of the evil one.

Let him hear—that *we* cannot do the judging.

Let him hear—that the righteous will shine. The words for the weeds are darkness and fire. The word for those made righteous by Christ is light.

Let him hear—that the judgment offers reward as well as punishment. Sons (and daughters) of the kingdom have nothing to fear in the judgment; in fact, they have everything to hope for. This used to bother the late H. G. Wells, who insisted that the promise of heaven with its pearly gates and golden streets was too much of an enticement to righteousness. He preferred to be good—for nothing.[3] Of course he wasn't, but that is perhaps beside the point. Wells notwithstanding, Jesus does not hesitate to promise that "the righteous will shine like the sun in the kingdom of their Father."

Let him hear—that Christ makes us righteous. The parable begins with the work of the sower. The good seed does not make itself good, and neither do the sons of the kingdom. Their sins are wiped out and they are made righteous by the gracious forgiveness of the Son of man. They are good in relation to Christ, not in themselves.

This reminder is necessary, for many look forward to the judgment day with anxiety, believing that on the day God will weigh their good deeds against their evil deeds and accept them into heaven or condemn them to hell on the basis of the balance. Return, however, to Jesus' words on the judgment in John 12. Verse 46 indicates (as do many other Scriptures) that belief, not works, is the basis of the judgment: "I have come as light into the world, that whoever *believes* in me may not remain in darkness." (See also John 11:25, John 3:16-18, John 6:28, 29, Acts 16:30-34—and many, many others.) It is true that some will be condemned because their works are evil, and no pretended belief can save them (Matthew 7:21-23). It is true also that genuine belief in Christ moves us to do good and not evil (James 2:26). But sometimes we do wrong, even if our belief is real (Romans 7:19). The crowning, triumphant truth is this: If our belief in Christ is genuine, our sins are not only forgiven, but forgotten. They do not figure in the final judgment at all (Romans 8:1).

In Charlotte Bronte's famous novel *Jane Eyre,* Mr. Brockelhurst, the headmaster of Lowood School, lectures Jane about her conduct. To frighten her into submissive behavior, he asks her questions about hell, concluding, "And what must you do to avoid it?"

"I must keep in good health and not die," she innocently answers him.

A reasonable answer. But impossible to accomplish, of course. One day Jane, like the rest of us, will die.

What then?

Notes

1. Quoted in Edward Fudge, "Putting Hell in Its Place." *Christianity Today.* August 6, 1976, p. 14.
2. Taken from *The Dust of Death* by Os Guinness. © 1973 by IVCF and used by permission of InterVarsity Press.
3. Paul Scherer, *Love Is a Spendthrift.* New York: Harper and Row Publishers, © 1961, p. 184.